Engaging Heaven for Revelation

Volume 2

More Riches from Heaven

By

Dr. Ron M. Horner

Engaging Heaven for Revelation
Volume 2

More Riches from Heaven

By

Dr. Ron M. Horner

LifeSpring International Ministries
PO Box 5847
Pinehurst, North Carolina 28374
www.RonHorner.com

Engaging Heaven for Revelation – Volume 2

More Riches from Heaven

Copyright © 2023 Dr. Ron M. Horner

Scripture is taken from the New King James Version®. Copyright © 1982 by Thomas Nelson. Used by permission. All rights reserved. (Unless otherwise noted.)

Scripture marked (TPT) is taken from The Passion Translation Copyright ©2017, 2018 by Passion & Fire Ministries, Inc. Used by permission. All rights reserved. ThePassionTranslation.com

Scripture marked (THE MIRROR) is taken from The Mirror Study Bible by Francois du Toit. Copyright © 2021 All Rights Reserved. Used by permission of the author.

Scripture marked (ARTB) is taken from the Ancient Roots Translinear Bible by Frances Werner. Copyright © 2005, 2006. 2011. Used by permission of the author.

All rights reserved. This book is protected by the copyright laws of the United States of America. This book may not be copied or reprinted for commercial gain or profit. The use of short quotations or occasional page copying for personal, or group study is permitted and encouraged. Permission granted upon request.

Any trademarks mentioned or used are the property of their respective owners.

Requests for bulk sales discounts, editorial permissions, or other information should be addressed to:

LifeSpring Publishing
PO Box 5847
Pinehurst, NC 28374 USA

Additional copies available at www.courtsofheaven.net

ISBN 13 TP: 978-1-953684-34-9
ISBN 13 eBook: 978-1-953684-35-6

Cover Design by Darian Horner Design
(www.darianhorner.com)
Image: #137529428 (123rf.com)

First Edition: May 2023

10 9 8 7 6 5 4 3 2 1

Printed in the United States of America

Table of Contents

Acknowledgements i
Preface iii
Characters Mentioned vii
Chapter 1 Living by the Spirit 1
Chapter 2 Engaging Our Senses 13
Chapter 3 Turning the Tables.. 23
Chapter 4 Freedom from Slavery...................................... 35
Chapter 5 Wellsprings in South America 41
Chapter 6 Erecting Shields and Governing Realms 45
Chapter 7 It is Time for Joy... 55
Chapter 8 Utilizing Keys 65
Chapter 9 Reverse Covenants Within Contracts 69
Chapter 10 Relationships & Trades................................. 77
Chapter 11 The Discipline of Our Soul........................... 85
Chapter 12 Collapsing Storms 97
Chapter 13 The Good Shepherd 113
Chapter 14 Observing Traffic Patterns 117
Chapter 15 The Outpouring
   & Removing the Filters on the Mind........................ 123

Chapter 16 Embracing Change.. 135
Chapter 17 A Word About Surrender 139
Chapter 18 Abraham on Surrender 147
Chapter 19 Angelic Engagement................................... 151
Chapter 20 Shifting Paradigms 155
Chapter 21 Encouragement to Believe 161
Chapter 22 Rise Up!.. 165
Chapter 23 The Angel of Inventory............................... 173
Chapter 24 Our Living Calendar 175
Chapter 25 New Angelic Tools 177
Chapter 26 The Eye Salve 183
Chapter 27 Working with Our Assignments 189
Chapter 28 Epilogue.. 199
Appendix 201
Learning to Live Spirit First 201
Works Cited... 209
Description 211
About the Author 213
Other Books by Dr. Ron M. Horner............................. 215

Acknowledgements

Thanks to the awesome Courts of Heaven team who work tirelessly to see people brought to freedom through the Courts of Heaven and engagements with Heaven. Thanks also to my audience and supporters. May the blessings of Heaven overflow in your life.

Preface

The icebreaker ship on the cover of the first volume was not only appropriate, but also prophetic. We were breaking the ice in certain arenas with what was shared in that volume, and we will continue breaking the ice in this volume. There are some characteristics of ice that need to be recognized as being common to religion and religious thought. First: it is cold; much of religion is cold and uninviting. Second: it is unforgiving; should we fall on ice, it is quite possible we will experience injury. Religion is not very forgiving either. Third: ice must be exposed to a different climate to change. That sounds a lot like religion, doesn't it? Only in the light of the Son will religious thoughts experience change. May we allow the climate of Heaven to change us.

It helps us when we understand that revelation always tests the quality of the soil in which it is sown. Whether it will bring forth a harvest depends upon the quality of the soil as well as the light and water it receives as the seed germinates and bursts forth through the soil. Whether it becomes a small, insignificant plant or a mighty tree depend on those factors as well as the light to which it is exposed. One of the ways we can gain more from the things shared in this book is to be sure that we are positioned spirit-forward, instructing our soul to simply rest. Since revelation must first land in the realm of our spirit, our soul is not qualified for the revelation itself. Revelation is not *FOR* the soul, although the soul will benefit. Revelation is for the growth of our *spirit*. After receiving revelation, our spirit can communicate to our soul what it needs to know and understand from the revelation that has been shared.

Do we understand everything contained in the seeds of a revelation? No. We do not pretend to, but we do intend to glean from the revelation and ask Heaven to continue to unfold to us more of the riches of Heaven. A principle unveiled to me was...

---

*The truth I embrace
is the truth from which I can benefit.*

Our mind (as part of our soul) is in the process of being renewed so that it thinks in line with the realms of Heaven.

It is not a requirement that our soul be able to grasp revelation that is spiritual in nature. Help our soul to understand this by speaking to our soul in a manner like this:

> *Soul, it is OK for you to not understand this revelation yet. Understanding will come but allow my spirit within to gain the revelation first. Do not*

try to do double duty by being a soul and a spirit when you are only a soul. Your job right now is to rest and let my spirit lead. I instruct you to step back and allow my spirit to come to the forefront.

Spirit, I speak to you and call you to come forward to the forefront. Glean from Heaven all that is being revealed, then communicate to my soul what you have learned in a manner that it can understand.

This should aid us in maximizing the revelation contained in this book. We will discover new weapons and strategies to use against the enemy. Heaven also unveiled some of the strategies of Satan against people and organizations. We received instruction concerning various means of protection, and we learned so many more things.

Find a quiet place and sit down and enjoy the information in this volume. May revelation and the Spirit of Revelation visit with us as we read.

Invite our angel(s) to assist us as we read to keep distractions minimized and help keep our mind focused. We have begun a journey that will propel us in our walk with God. Enjoy the journey!

———·———

Characters Mentioned

We make mention of several different characters who assist us to unpack this revelation, including:

Alicia – A woman in white who is our Personnel Director

Ezekiel – the chief angel over LifeSpring International Ministries

Garzan – One of Ezekiel's commanding angels

George – a man in white who is our Finance Advisor

Lydia – a woman in white linen who often teaches and advises us from Heaven

Malcolm – a man in white linen who often teaches and advises us from Heaven

Mitchell – a man in white linen who also instructs us.

Chapter 1
Living by the Spirit

Wind currents are blowing that our spirits need to become sensitive to. These currents are both spiritual and natural. The writer of Hebrews wrote, "He makes his spirits winds, his ministers a flame of fire," (Hebrews 1:7). Mitchell had some things to discuss with us.

A current is flowing from Heaven through our spirit man that we can get in, like on the back of a kite and we could flow with that wind. This is a spirit forward activity.

From our spirit man we choose the wind (or winds) we want to receive from. These winds are ministering angels released to the dimension of the earth. **They must be received *from* the spirit *in* the spirit.** They come near to assist with the lifting or the raising up of the spirit to a current that is not the present current of earth or not the present current of the soul realm.

> *Earth operates on the soul realm through the interaction of humanity.*

But spirits awakened by God have opportunity to ascend to different currents being released from Heaven and remain in those currents. This is a spiritual activity. A spiritual activity is one of *focus* where we become aware of where our spirit man could potentially focus. We must direct our spirit to that place.

> *The soul needs to understand what the spirit knows.*

It needs to get training from the spirit of man. The spirit of man gets training; it receives comfort, peace, joy and is watered by and fed by the Holy Spirit from the Kingdom realm. However, the enemy of our soul hopes we never find this avenue, even if we are born again, so that our spirit man is not filled by the Holy Spirit or awakened to gain strength to flip our manner of life to spirit forward living—spirit first living.

The soul is often adjudicating things from the physical realm based on intellect and emotion and memory—these memories are often linked to mindsets of youthful experiences. The soul realm can be functioning well in the 3-D world, but the component of the spirit is imperative for spirit life.

An awakened spirit hears from God. An awakened spirit hungers for the things of God. An awakened spirit can be hungry, thirsty, in need of fellowship, in need of love, and in need of companionship. These are the things our spirit man has need of. Many people get these confused with their soul and often their soul is confused with their spirit.

Our spirit is a realm filled by the power of God, filled by companionship with Jesus, companionship with the Father, companionship with Holy Spirit. Our spirit is the receiver of the seven spirits of God and their functionality and what they are releasing. Our spirit is the light that causes other spirits to be touched and awakened. Thus, ministry from the spirit is much better than ministry from the soul.

> *For the power of God to be released into the earth, the spirit of the man must be engaged to receive that power and might of the Holy Spirit and direct it. It must be directed.*

It can be directed in intercession. It can be directed in conversation. It can be directed through the body by the laying on of hands, but all these things are sourced from the spirit of the person. The soul and the spirit have been redeemed unto the Father. The Father's pleasure is that our spirit is in communion with Him, His Son, Holy Spirit, Heaven, and those dwelling now in the Kingdom of God.

We call these the great cloud of witnesses such as Mitchell. He is one of those. Our discipline of relationship is to be childlike, hungry, thirsty, and willing.

The enemy will often use the will of the soul to interrupt what the spirit is willing to do. This takes discipline, practice, and feeding on the Word of God to know one's identity as spirit-first in order to overcome the resistance that the enemy is using within the soul realm.

Many beliefs exist in mankind currently. It has not always been this way, but it is right now. There are many soul realm distractions and edifications—the things that our soul goes to or turns to get edified; these include everything from excitement to food. There are some good things that our soul will allow itself to receive from. These are not necessarily bad, Rather, they are out of balance, and if not aligned properly with the spirit and the way the spirit experiences this, we are not living in our full identity or at our full capacity.

The life of Jesus has much to be studied to look between the lines and allow Holy Spirit to teach us how Jesus lived as a man with an awakened spirit in conjunction with Holy Spirit and with the flow of might and power of the authority of the Kingdom of God. Notice this was even before he went to the cross for the payment of all sin. So too were the disciples and the seventy released, first being taught who they were and then they were released with many instructions. The instructions we read in the scripture are just a few of them. What they did was they walked in the spirit, trusting the power and might of the flow of the Holy Spirit (within their spirit), along with winds and currents to heal the sick and carry out many authorities against the enemy. (Luke 10:1-24)

We were recently shown the three realms of a person in a straight line with the bridges between the three inner realms with the soul in the middle, and it was pointed out to us how a healing anointing may get stuck in the soul. Holy Spirit calls that which is in the soul that gets in the way "mind genuflections."[1] Our mind and our soul is bowing down to a preconceived notion or something we thought. Instead of surrendering to that, do not bow down, do not pay homage to that thing we were taught, but allow healing to flow through the conduit of the soul to our body realm so that the body realm receives what the might and power of God is releasing.

The phrase "mind genuflection" is such an interesting phrase because we get that picture of a person bowing down to an idol or to a religious tradition or to something they thought that they have just not rethought, or they had not surrendered to the potential for a rethinking on it. We are walking in such an age of that right now with portions of the Body of Christ being assisted in new thoughts about that. We are learning to rethink a great many things—particularly concerning religious traditions.

---

[1] Genuflection—a bowing of the knee

Mitchell told us that he is not too concerned that we struggle so hard to get some of this understanding. He is confident that this is all coming out in the perfect timing of God. Just the sowing of seed to people regarding their spirit being and getting them thinking about the different operations of their being is breaking off religiosity and religious thinking and helping them to begin to really consider how personal one's spirit can be with the personality of the Son, the Father, and the Holy Spirit.

When we move from the place of living from our spirit, nothing is impossible. It is the atmosphere of Heaven. When we move in that realm and we teach our soul to sit down and rest because we are going to operate from the place that has no impossibility, we are going to eventually connect that to how it manifests in the earth.

Dwell on these things in the realm of the current of winds where nothing is impossible. Dwell in a current of joy, a current of abundance, a current of blessing, a current of building, a current of creativity. These are winds released from Heaven. Let us receive these winds into our spirit realm. Tell our soul to be affected by this spirit realm and by what the spirit realm knows as it is affected by the currents in which it is flowing.

At this point, Ezekiel appeared and joined Mitchell in instructing us.

Get into winds of being comfortable, speaking to angels, learning from angels, partnering with angels, engaging angels in the spirit of the things they do well. Our soul can be concerned with something Heaven is not concerned about and when we feed that part of our soul and we feed on those concerns that Heaven is not concerned with, our attention and our focus is very easily and quickly shifted to look and live from the natural realm.

Living from the natural realm is problem oriented. It is solution oriented.

> *Living from the spirit realm*
> *is not solution oriented.*
> *It is possibility oriented.*

It is "nothing is impossible oriented." It is not finding a solution; it is *receiving* the solution. Believers have walked in a grace for a long time, where without knowing their spirit was helping them, they were receiving creative ideas and understanding. It is not like this is brand new, but the potential and the opportunity and the increasing greatness of it is.

Operating from Our Spirit

Our thinking is that it would be so much simpler to do all of this from the spirit and not get stuck in the soul where the soul begins to feel weary. We can say to our soul, "We may feel weary because we are trying to do something that we are not meant to do. We are going to step over to the spirit realm. We are going to let our spirit lead, and we are going to fly through these activities. We are going to be assisted. We are going to have angels speak to us and have the Kingdom of God participating with us."

This happens from the spirit man. Do not worry. It is just a matter of learning to practice that—learning that it is available and then learning to do it and to stay in it. That is what the winds help with and help us stay in it and stay on it.

Letting Our Soul Operate

We will have times for our soul to be an operation. For example, if a feast in the physical realm is being prepared, we need our soul to engage the fellowship of the feast, the taste of the food, the flow of the conversation, the enjoyment of the moment.

Now, imagine that in the same scenario where we are engaged with our spirit as well. Our spirit does not necessarily take the first position but assists the soul in processing what is going on. Some call this looking beyond, looking between the lines, looking with spirit sight, or looking in the spirit to see what also is taking place. Then from this position, we see angels, we feel them, we taste the river of God, the goodness of His participation with us at the feast (I am talking about a physical feast). When we do things this way, is not our enjoyment much more magnified because we have engaged the soul *AND* the spirit realm, because Father made us this way? If we ever feel in a stuck place, engage to see which realm we are operating out of and switch to the other, and then agree that they can communicate. We can do both—we can live from both.

Flesh is the Flesh

Flesh is the flesh. I am talking about the body side of our beings. The flesh is always going to follow what the soul and spirit are doing, believing what the soul believes. If it is not in second place, behind what the spirit is feeding upon, then there is a manifestation of the flesh that is behind the other two realms. Therefore, if a belief system in our spirit is communicated to our soul, and our soul agrees, surrendering to the belief of the spirit, then the body benefits by receiving from the soul what it has agreed with in the spirit, and it will manifest, but it will take time to manifest in the physical realm. It does not happen instantly. Very often it happens in what we would call a gradual manner, but it does happen. We can look for it. Many are impatient, expecting the physical realm to operate in the same parameter of timelessness that the spirit operates in, but we must be patient and kind to our flesh.

Let me give an example. Our soul has recognized from our spirit a need to change our diet. I am talking about the natural food we put in our body. The soul must first go through a phase where it is willing to surrender the things that it has believed, whether incorrect information about nutrition, or whether it is just emotional conditioning to the things that are not healthy. As the soul aligns with new patterns of thought, we can get the spirit involved. The spirit will help the soul stay in that realm of a changed mindset and eventually we will find ourselves feeding our body differently, and from that, the body will eventually benefit. This is a common thing to talk about, but we may not have seen it from the three realms of which we are comprised.

Our Spirit and Worship

The spirit has the capacity to see itself like the Father.

This next thing I will share is linked to worship. It is linked to why we worship. Our spirit worships in that **it focuses upon where it came from, what it truly is, and who is responsible for that**, which would be the Creator. It would be the Almighty God. It would be the living resurrected one. The spirit worships because it receives benefit and empowerment by focusing spiritual senses on the character of God from which one's spirit came. Is this not truly seeing who we are?

Worship helps us see who we are by seeing who He is.

Struggling to See

People who struggle with identity issues often struggle with worship because they are using the wrong eyes to determine their identity. They are using natural eyes to try to determine who they are instead of their spiritual eyes to see who *He* is, and to see us mirrored in a reflection of who He is. To see which facet of Him we are most like comes from spirit activity of praise, worship, relationship, companionship, affection for the spirit realm, for the Godhead, for the unseen.

Fear in Hearing

I frequently ask people to journal and wondered why they often would not. Heaven explained that they are afraid they are going to hear something negative. They do *not* hear something negative, but they are afraid that they are going to hear something negative, and they believe this in their soul, and it shuts down their spirit from hearing. The needed work is the cleansing of the soul.

> *If the soul does not communicate the power and might of God to the body, it is because the soul has fragments.*

It has broken places. It has woundedness. It has fear—it contains fear. Fear is like a lens or a great veil over the spirit, and the true flow of the spirit is not released correctly because it gets distorted through the veil (of fear) that is in the soul. This is why the cleansing of the bloodline, the cleansing of mindsets, and the alignment of letting the spirit guide our understanding is so crucial.

The soul is made to work in the 3-D realm. It is not made to work in spiritual matters and seeing matters.

But there is plenty of help for us—the angels, cloud of witnesses, Holy Spirit, Jesus, Father; all these voices help us see all these things, to experience all these things, to encounter not from our soul realm, but from our spirit realm. This is for every believer who chooses to walk into the discovery of this relationship. In this hour, there are countless scales falling off many eyes.

———·———

Chapter 2
Engaging Our Senses

Comparison can be our downfall. We had noticed that some who follow our ministry would compare their ability to see to someone else's ability.

The Father gives freely to all who ask and increases the gifting as the recipient practices with what they have been given. For those who have been given a small amount to practice with what they have, soon will be given a larger amount if they are faithful with the small amount. These things come by "the process of degree," like a small percentage of advancement each time the recipient is engaged in receiving the access to the Kingdom of God, through Jesus Christ.

The recipient who stands at the door, moans, and complains that they cannot enter in has not actually put their foot forward to step in.

They must have a renewing of the mind. They must have a mental understanding that Jesus *has* given access. Therefore, they can access often.

> *It is their mind believing lies from*
> *Satan that keeps them from*
> *the boldness, the courage,*
> *and the activity of the engagement.*

Therefore, it helps when I say, "Now we are going to step into the realms of Heaven. And now we are going to write. We are going to experience and engage Heaven and when we step out of Heaven, we are going to write down what Heaven is saying." This puts a demand on the people. They feel they have been given permission. They feel they are not doing it alone. They feel they are doing it under the tutelage of one who has understanding and practice. Therefore, the demand equates to ability in their mind, and they do not wonder *if* they can accomplish this; they simply accomplish it. Another way to say this, is 'they *become* it. They *are* it.' The English language does not really serve here, but they answer the invitation under the beckoning of the tutelage that I have released when I say, "Now we're going to do this."

Sometimes we must help each other. You could even say, "Picture in your soul's imagination me (Dr. Ron) saying, 'Now we are going to step in,'" and then do it as if I am there before you, and you are doing it and writing what is being perceived from Heaven. After three or four minutes, what our engagement would have been was increased because I put a demand on the gift, which causes the gift to expand.

> *Everyone should be able to hear and
> to see when their mind is renewed.*

We have this access and indeed, this is our identity—beings who commune. Is this not what Adam was created to do, to be a being who communes with the Godhead? This relationship of communion has been reopened by the Son and His overwhelming triumph over every resistance and contrary spirit of darkness.

Let me talk about a problem. There are many among us who are *more focused on the enemy* than they are on the Father. This is very regretful because they *shut down* their spiritual gifts and spiritual senses when they are more focused on the enemy. This is because...

> *When we focus on the enemy,
> we are looking at fear—
> we are focused on fear.*

We are not focused on love, or what the Father has given us, or what our access truly is.

> *Where we are focusing our mind
> is where we will see.*

If we are seeing tremendously terrible scenes, we are not looking at the Father, we are looking at the enemy. Repent so that we may have our eyes opened to see His Glory realm.

I realize how blunt this is, but this is not the fault of the individuals. This is the result of the fact that we do not have many fathers, and when we lack fathers teaching their children in the natural, it equates to incorrect foundations within that person. Many have not had fathers teaching them the foundations of spiritual access to the Kingdom of God, even since the resurrection of Jesus. [1 Corinthians 4:14-16 (TPT)]

We have many things we need to be seeing. Some need to see the Father and how loving He is. Some need to see the Son, Jesus, and how affectionate He is. Some need to see the angels of God in the heavenly realm and how capable they are. Some need to see the beauty of the Glory of His presence. Yet, some are stepping in and getting waylaid.

Recall how, in previous seasons, what it felt like to our flesh when the anointing fell, or when the presence of the Holy Spirit was very evident—the flesh feels it. We call this the "heavy weight of His Glory." We are using the <u>soul</u> and the <u>flesh</u> to discern the spirit realm because the Holy Spirit is tangible.

However, as we grow up into mature sons and daughters of the Kingdom, having been given access through the veil through Jesus' own blood and body, we are engaging Heaven's presence and its Glory in a different way. Now we use <u>soul</u> *and* <u>spirit</u>. Notice that when we step into the realms of Heaven using spiritual sight and spiritual ears, our flesh is not feeling because we are not engaging the flesh realm. We are engaging the soul and spirit realm. However, even the soul's aspect of that engagement is much reduced.

---

*The spirit of man has the capacity
to have the mind of Christ,
which has emotional capacities
in spiritual terms.*

For instance, when we have seen into the spirit and we have seen a lovely pastoral scene of a green hillside, and we have seen the Shepherd sitting there—Jesus—we have engaged Him. Have we not felt His affection? Have we not felt his love? These are manifestations of the spirit realm, that the *spirit* of man is capable of understanding. What our soul is doing is interpreting that to our mind, but our spirit is fully engaged there too.

We must welcome and abide in that place with the activation of all our spiritual senses. As most people are stepping into the realms of Heaven, they are not understanding that they already *are* using all their five spiritual senses. If we concentrate on what is *not* at work or what we do *not* have working, we are going to limit what *is* working. So...

---

*If we step into the spiritual realm
and we hear, or we sense,
we can turn our spiritual eyes
to that and open them.*

Many are abandoning the process before they have paused enough in stillness to see what happens. Like children, they demand instant and immediate comprehension when there is a process of gradually pausing in the presence and allowing the engagement of Heaven to become more real, and more seen, heard, felt, tasted, and touched. The Body of Christ is growing up in this.

What We Have to Offer

Lydia appeared to share some things related to the men and women in white linen, of which she is one.

She wanted to talk about what they have to offer as the great cloud of witnesses. Regarding this, there are many of God's people in Heaven who have specific assignments to bring about the manifestation of His Glory. Sometimes these will be termed miracles, but this is also just the working out of the destinies of both those on earth and those in Heaven where their destinies mesh to bring about the fullness of the Kingdom of God. It is going to begin happening in greater measure in days ahead because the bride of Christ is learning who she is.

Where we have fully embraced that we have been given full access in Jesus Christ and that all His children have full access, we begin the journey—one of hunger and thirst to know more of His Kingdom and to know Him better, to know what He has in store for us. In some ways, even those in the cloud of witnesses (those we call men and women dressed in white), have their destinies tied to ours as well. We are all bringing about the Glory of God in His creation.

Not all the men and women in white linen have assignments to those on earth. There are other assignments in Heaven, and do not forget, they have a great capacity to engage the celebratory events of Heaven. But many of the cloud of witnesses who engage with those of earth (us) as part of what they are assigned to from the Father's Heavenly Kingdom realm, they delight to do this. Therefore, what we have learned and have been taught in the Business Complex of Heaven is what has been made available to the saints. In these days, there are many things that Heaven is going to manifest through the sons and daughters of God alive in the earth realm as they seek counsel from the great cloud of witnesses and from God's angels.

The more we concentrate on the Kingdom of God, the more the enemy trembles, but mostly he gnashes his teeth because we are not paying attention to him. We have learned to pay attention to truth, and to the delight of Heaven, and to relationship with the Godhead. The enemy is like a fly that we are no longer even worried by because we simply have chosen not to give it attention. The enemy simply gnashes his teeth when he does not have our attention.

Why do we think he tempts? He tempts in a twisted manner to gain our attention and thus our worship. It is an attempt to gain our worship.

> *When we focus on him, he equates
> this to his own worship.*

Angels have been given leave to take care of unseen spirits, and the evil spirits, evil, and the spirits of evil men. Angels have been given assignment to these things.

Our destiny is to pray as led by Holy Spirit and to engage the realms of Heaven, that we might find what Heaven is revealing that Heaven wants earth to reflect by this.

> *We WILL build the Kingdom of God
> on earth, as it is in Heaven.*

If we had a tuning fork and we struck that tuning fork, if a stringed instrument is in the room, it will begin to resonate the same frequency without us ever striking the instrument simply because we have struck the tuning fork in the same space. That is a resonance. That is the Spirit of the Lord in the spirits of many.

> *We are designed to resonate
> with the Glory realm.*

We are *not* designed to resonate with Satan's realm or Satan's so-called kingdom, but we must tune to the Father's frequency. We must tune to Heaven. We must be focused on Heaven, searching with belief and faith that we will hear, see, feel, taste, and touch."

Believe it or not, the soul is at rest when we are in the spirit realm accomplishing these things from our spirit. Is this not the access that Jesus afforded to us? Then the soul translates to the flesh what it has felt from the spirit of the person who has engaged with the heavenly realm.

It felt as if we had been given a bag of gemstones or a bag of gold, but what we really received is a bag of spectacles—lenses to view from.

Chapter 3
Turning the Tables

We are aware that some of the revelations we release are contrary to religion and religious tradition. Recently, following one of our Mentoring Classes, we became aware of a variety of accusations that were being tossed about in the atmosphere and were creating a battle of sorts.

The accusation in the atmosphere was that we are leading people astray.

- All this talk about talking to angels, don't we know this is how error creeps into the church and we should not be teaching babies to talk to angels because don't we know this is how cults get started?
- We are being irresponsible to teach children to do these things because we are going to be the reason they get in trouble—we are!

- Remember that Joseph Smith spoke to an angel and the Mormon church was the result. If we teach people that they can talk to angels, we are opening the door for the enemy to persecute the church through a belief system that is not true.
- We are doing this terrible thing telling people they should talk to angels.

All of these were fear-based reasons saying that people will fall into error.

Jesus dealt with a similar thing and spoke of it in Luke 11:52-54:

"You are nothing but hopeless frauds, you experts of religion! You take away from others the key that opens the door to the house of knowledge. Not only do you lock the door and refuse to enter, but you also do your best to keep others from the truth."

The religious leaders and experts of the law became enraged and began to furiously oppose him. They harassed Jesus all the way out the door, spewing out their hostility, arguing over everything he said—wanting nothing more than to find a reason to entrap him with his own words.

In The Mirror Translation[2] it reads:

Shame on you. Professors of religious rules and regulations. You have placed the key of knowledge beyond anyone's reach. You yourself have never even opened the door to this realm. And have kept anyone who desired to dwarfed inside your own little world. (THE MIRROR)

Jesus was talking to them because they were pestering him with questions about "How can you do this?" That verse holds quite a lot when we truly peer into what the verse is really saying. It is eye-opening. Even in that day, they understood some things that they were guarding for themselves and not sharing with the people. We had been aware in our spirit that the previous night, a person bound in religion joined us as a participant on our Tuesday Night Mentoring Class. We could sense in the spirit many accusations being leveled toward us. We did not want these accusations left unanswered, so we took them to the Courts of Heaven.

Father, we thank You today for access to the Mercy Court in the name of Jesus. We thank You Father that You gave Jesus to us, that we might enter Your

---

[2] Much criticism has been leveled toward Francois duToit for his translation of the Bible. While we may not concur with everything he believes or teaches, we have found much richness in much of his translation and commentary. It provides a freshness that is beneficial to our Christian walk. Allow Holy Spirit to be our ultimate teacher.

courts today and we enter boldly with praise upon our lips with affection for You Father.

We desire to agree with our adversary quickly, according to Matthew 5:25, to get free of the accusations leveled against us:

We are leading people astray,

We, with all our talk of angels, are leading are causing error to creep into the church,

We should not be teaching babies to talk to angels,

We are starting a cult

or

We are positioning people to fall to error and to start a cult.

We answer the accusation:

That we are being irresponsible to teach children to speak to angels because we are going to get them in trouble, or we are going to be the reason they get in trouble.

We specifically address the accusation that we are operating as Joseph Smith did in speaking to an angel, or that we are proposing that people speak to angels of darkness hidden and disguised in light. And...

> We are opening the door for the enemy to persecute the church,
>
> We are teaching belief systems that are not true, and
>
> We are causing people to fall into error.
>
> We are doing something bad by helping people understand that they can talk to angels.
>
> Father, we agree with the accuser, according to Matthew 5:25.
>
> We confess this as sin, and we repent for it in the name of Jesus, and we ask for the blood of the lamb to cover this.
>
> If we have operated in this in any degree Father, we would not want to do that. We would confess that it would be sin, and so we ask that the blood of Jesus would cover that.

We were then informed that we were to add an amendment to this case:

> As we receive forgiveness (and thank You for it). We ask that the human that is bound by religious spirits that just tuned into the Zoom meeting last night, we ask that this human would be ministered to by the Spirit of Truth, that their eyes would be opened, that they would know You, they would know Your realm.
>
> We ask for an amendment of this case that— whether one or more humans on our call last

night, Father—that You would meet them with such love in Your Kingdom. That they would see their alignment with a religious spirit and would be freed from that. We ask this in Jesus' name.

Yes, we forgive the human who has these thoughts in their realm and who invited that religious spirit into the meeting. We forgive them as we have been forgiven and we bless them and release them from their guilt in the name of Jesus.

We also repent Father and confess as sin according to our accuser—we meet our accuser with the accusation that we are out of balance. Father, we confess that being out of balance is sin. Where if we have engaged in being out of balance, Father, we repent for that, confess it as sin and ask the blood of Jesus to cover that.

Thank You. Jesus.

Father, as another amendment to this case, we request on behalf of the human that was in our meeting last night that opened the door to this religious and Pharisaical spirit, Father, we request that in this court case, we request—

We were made to understand that there was someone among us the prior evening who had great fear and that this fear had opened the door to the Pharisee spirit. We were told we had the opportunity to engage a court case like an amendment to the prior case regarding that person and request freedom from fear for them.

Father, we attach as an amendment to this court case and request that You would hear our testimony as we forgive this person who is watching our live broadcast with us. We forgive that person for agreeing with fear. We bless them and release them in Jesus' name. We ask that they be delivered from the spirit of fear by being shown the Spirit of Truth.

More understanding came that because of this fear and the spirit of fear that this person had, it opened the door to the spirit of the Pharisee and that others in the meeting were having to battle that and they did not know what it was, but they were perceiving it too.

We asked what we could ask for against the enemy that the court would judge upon?

Father, due to our repentance and our willingness to forgive this one who was aligned with the fear and the spirit of the Pharisee, we ask of this court that You would flip the outcome—hat where the spirit of fear and the spirit of the Pharisee wanted to infect the hearers and the seers and affect their heart, that You would release from Heaven miracles, signs, and wonders to the effect that these individuals who were forced against their will to battle against this, that their angels would be given signs, wonders, and miracles that they might know themselves as sons and daughters of the Most High. We ask this as an amendment to this court case in Jesus' name, that they would overwhelmingly know, understand, and perceive the truth, and the love of God for them more abundantly than ever and as they receive this in their heart it brings about a mind shift so that they know that they know their belief in this ability to access the realms of heaven, to speak to angelic beings of the Lord of Hosts and gain truth, and that they would overwhelmingly know the love of God in this. We request this in Jesus' name.

Thank You, Father, for the help of Your Court.

Thank You. Holy Spirit for Your counsel.

Thank You, Father, for Your power.

We agree with the release of the angels to their work.

Our request was granted with a lot of celebration within the court by those present.

Ezekiel explained to us that the previous night on the mentoring call, there was a battlefield that he and his ranks were in. This morning, he requested mirrors. He requested this for those who have engaged the angelic angels assigned to them to collaborate with he and his ranks. Many more of our listeners have commissioned their angels to network with Ezekiel, his commanders, and ranks. Ezekiel desired that the angels be equipped with mirrors, to work with the angels of the people to mirror to them reflections of themselves as sons and daughters of the Father.

> *Heaven wants us to know
> how alike we are to the Father.*

He delights that we are created in His image, redeemed by His Son, and growing in our sonship. These mirrors will assist those who have chosen alignment with the ministry to receive this.

> *Satan works against the church
> by coming with torments, lies,
> and skirmishes and he will use
> anyone who is aligned with fear
> to bring this sort of thing about.*

What really began to form with the courtroom work we did was our forgiving those people aligned with fear. The Father, the court, and the counselors of the court all wanted us to use this moment to launch an offensive against the enemy so that those people get freedom, so they get truth. They get another chance. They get the love of the Father. What we did flipped what the enemy did on his head.

One of the great ironies I have noticed is that the more we strive to *not* be in error, the more likely we are to be found in error. The problem arises when we decide that we must be the judge of everything we hear or read when the ultimate judge is God, our Father. Our judgments are likely to be coming from the Tree of the Knowledge of Good and Evil and *not* from the Tree of

Life. Therefore, when we start with the wrong source, we will end up with the wrong result.

> *The more we strive, the less we are resting in the care of our Father to take care of us, to protect us from harm, and to teach us.*

I, in my wisdom, as great as I might think I am, I am not qualified to be the arbiter of truth for anyone. Nor is anyone else. Let us allow Holy Spirit to do what he has been doing well for thousands of years: allow Him to be our teacher. He will guide us into all truth—John 16:13.

The Beauty of Seclusion

Ezekiel had one more tip he wanted to share and that is **the beauty of seclusion in the process of learning access to the realms of Heaven**. Sometimes on our own, people are attempting to step into Heaven, but they have not found their place of a distraction-free atmosphere. That is on two levels.

> *As we are learning our spirit's capacity to engage Heaven, we are going to need a prayer closet.*

We are going to need a space where we are not at risk of being interrupted and where we can get very quiet. A lot of chaos exists in the atmospheres of many people, and they are not taking the time at the beginning to quiet themselves down to seek the solitude. They are expecting to do this on the go, and while we may be able to do this on the go as we have matured in it, when we are young in this and learning, we need a quiet, distraction-free space. I am talking physically oriented here. We need to get alone. We need to be still. We need to be quiet. That is the first thing.

The second thing is many people are so filled. Their soul is so occupied with and filled with anxiety and worry about the future. These two things, *anxiety* and *worry* about the future within the soul, these are like a door closer to the spirit realm. We must park our soul. We must put it in neutral and...

Engage the spirit realm
from *our spirit*

Our soul's anxiety and worry about the future will not help us engage Heaven. It will hinder us.

The one who comes to the Father with the laundry list of burdens, anxieties, and worries must remember that the Father has already answered us in scripture. We are to cast these onto Jesus and enter in without these to receive help. Therefore, what we receive from Heaven often is the answer that the soul's anxieties and worries are searching for, but we must get it the right way. We cannot get it upside down. We have to say, "These are the anxieties of the world system and the burdens of living in the 3-D realm, but my soul *can* receive. My spirit can receive the answers by *spirit first*, and then I will communicate them to myself."

Now is the time for us to tell our soul to rest and be quiet and I *really* mean get *quiet*, because our soul is not used to doing this. Our soul will fight us on this when we begin; nevertheless, we will overcome, and our soul will learn to be quiet.

———·———

Chapter 4
Freedom from Slavery

Great effort has been made by the enemy to create racial divides in America. I was preparing to minister on the subject "Freedom from Slavery" and Heaven had some input for me. Malcolm explained that my meeting to talk about slavery was an important one because that topic is currently in the atmosphere of earth. It is very much a soul realm discussion. I was advised that what I needed to do was elevate it to a spiritual realm discussion and to do that, I would need permission from the audience. Those students listening would need to hear with their spirit man. They would need to engage with their spirit.

The effort it takes to calm the soul and be still so the spirit can come forward to engage this dynamic freedom that our Father in Heaven would give us—the effort is necessary for the completeness of the manifestation of that freedom in our nation.

This engagement with Heaven occurred in February which is designated Black History Month. Heaven described it as a soul realm label which invites the emotions to war against others' soul realms. We must be aware that Satan uses the soul realm against humanity to capture their thinking so that they may not receive the truth of the Father's Light, nor have their minds renewed to surrender the natural man's labels. We must release these labels to the Father so that he can renew our minds from the spirit; it is extremely necessary in this hour. Many people's souls are looking for freedom because they are keenly feeling the captivity.

Like we have pointed out many times, this captivity that the soul feels takes place in the skin suit of every color. Every color of skin has experienced captivity and slavery within the bloodlines and within the DNA and the epigenomes of human history and of humans in history. Therefore, this conversation is not a conversation about skin tone, but we must see that the enemy would use the natural man's label to stir up the soul so that the members of humanity erupt in violence in the physical realm,

It takes a great deal of shifting to the spirit realm and operating from *spirit forward living* in order to walk out a manifestation of grace toward all colors. This is done by *living spirit first* in conjunction with the infilling of the Holy Spirit's wisdom—the Spirit of Wisdom. The Spirit of Counsel must walk with our spirit regarding the false categories and the categorization of humanity based upon the color of one's skin. That is not to say that some categorization and its ensuing slavery has not occurred on the planet—it most certainly has.

As we recognize our own capacity for our soul to be enslaved, we can also have grace, love, and understanding for those whose bodies have been put in slavery conditions. To think about this from a spiritual standpoint is good because the resolution is not in the physical realm, it is in the spiritual realm.

While I teach on bloodlines caught in physical slavery, the spirit gets ahold of the truth and the light of this topic, and the individual becomes truly free from the spirit, first translating to the soul, which then it translates to the physical arena.

While it is true that there are not black slaves in America any longer, there *ARE* slaves in America as populations who have carried the soul fragmentation from physical slavery due to ancestors who *were* trapped in physical slavery. As the descendants of slaves get free within their spirit realm, they can begin enjoying courtroom work in the spirit before the Father, as sons and daughters of God, to conduct court cases that all slavery in the physical realm would cease and would come to an end.

First, getting free of the effects of the bloodline ancestry trapped in physical slavery will lead us to a greater propensity to pray about and operate in spiritual realms regarding setting people free who are captured in other manners—even in physical slavery. Work with what we know. Go from that. Address the segment of people that we have addressed and worked with in the past to set them free from the soul's slavery and the DNA of slavery.

Work with those in our sphere to gain freedom from American slavery, then counsel others that there is also a freedom they can receive from slavery. These include the island peoples.

The forces of evil put us in slavery and then they make us fight against others who were not our slave owners but are the purported slave owners.

---

*Slavery starts in the spirit realm.
We are first liberated in the
spirit realm and then our soul
can know rest from slavery.*

This is an ownership issue, and it has always been an ownership issue, because, while Yahweh created man, He did not create him to own another. He created man to know Him as sons and daughters, as a reflection of His beauty in the physical realm with whom He wanted to be family.

The idea of slavery is extremely anti-God. The idea of slavery is antichrist in nature. It is good for humanity to realize the broad strokes of slavery wherever it has manifested, in whatever age, and in whatever timeframe. Its basis is the lack of knowledge of God—not head knowledge, but its basis is not knowing that we are fathered and have a father. It is rebellion against fatherhood. It is not rooted in head knowledge. It is rooted in the soul's longing to be loved and accepted. The deception that fell on man when they felt separated from their purpose—this deception invited thrones and kingdoms into the earth realm to rule over humanity.

I know this is mysterious and I know you would like for me to bring this to you in a more logical manner. However, it is a walk of faith and understanding. Scripture tells us to walk in love with all men, because that is the nature of the Father in whose image we are created, and by whom we are created. Antichrist forces are at work against this knowledge. We are left where the soul does not understand the spirit that knows His love and, therefore, darkness is invited and captivity and slavery erupt.

I do not want to digress into too much broadness here because our first objective would be to help people be free from what is in their bloodline. The primary point that I am making here is that captivity and slavery has happened on both sides of the table. Whether we were captive in slavery, or whether we were the captor and the one who put people in slavery, *it is in all bloodlines on both sides.*

However, we must start somewhere, and starting with a recent thing such as American Black slavery would be beneficial. The goal here is for the soul and the body to wait. The goal is for the soul to feel comfort because freedom must come to the spirit first. Remember, the soul can translate to the body the freedom that it receives from the spirit. This is a type of renewing of the mind, the mind of our soul being renewed by the truth and the light received from the spiritual realm through courtroom work of spiritual dynamics that overturn long-standing verdicts against a people group.

Rejoicing is the response to freedom from captivity.

You may notice I use the word "slavery" and "captivity" interchangeably. This may help you understand that the principle aim of slavery is captivity, and it helps translate to a broader experience for people. Freedom is coming, and can come, and does come to those who engage the court cases and receive their freedom. Many sons and daughters are coming to God free from what has captured their minds, spirits, and hearts. This is a good thing as there is still work to do to eradicate slavery from the planet.

This engagement dealt with court work to gain freedom from slavery for those whose ancestors were slaves in America. Slavery is part of the history of every people group in one form or another. Access the Courts of Heaven and seek the path for freedom from slavery for ourselves and our bloodline. We offer a free course on our CourtsNet.com website called "Freedom from Slavery."

Chapter 5

Wellsprings in South America

In a debriefing meeting with Lydia, she had things to share concerning the Spanish Conference we had recently concluded.

She began, "A wellspring is taking place in the South American nations—the introduction of spirit forward living. These wellsprings are good. Some of these wellsprings are large, and some are very small fountains, but some will grow. Continue the work of the digging of the well so that the wellspring could flow unhindered and unblocked.

"For many of the people attending the meeting, the biggest cry of their heart was they felt alone, and they did not know how to flow by the spirit to instruct the soul to know that they are not alone. Many were to the point of being overwhelmed by religious ritual which holds no life. They felt lifeless in the soul realm because of the duties of what they were told to do in order to be a Christian.

"Many things are changing about this topic in the earth realm that the Father is releasing from Heaven. There are many nuances of winds and flames regarding the opening of the eye and the ear to understand how Christianity has become ritualized and captured by structures of man who do not follow the Holy Spirit. It is going to become evident in future days. The difference between those who follow the Holy Spirit, allowing Holy Spirit to work and lead, and those who have cold lifeless church buildings who are about to be frozen in their rigidity is going to become evident. When that occurs, their populations will leave them in droves," Lydia spoke.

The desire of the human heart to access the spirit of God in the intimate relationship that the Father has afforded through the Son is coming to planet earth and coming quickly. Where we see the movement of the river, we will need to address our spirit man—direct our spirit man—and give our spirit permission to flow there.

Satisfactions of the Spirit

How will mankind find the river of God as He pours out and releases it in this new era? They will hear of it and have ears to hear. They will see it and have eyes to see. And they will encounter a prompting and a leading by the hands of the heavenly host. These angels have been released to take individuals by the shoulders as if from behind and to direct them to where the river is flowing that they might go in and get wet. I am speaking on the spiritual plane, but I am also speaking on the physical plane. What has come to earth from recent events is the hunger of the spirit to get itself satisfied by the presence of God. As we know, the presence of God is sometimes the only satisfactory thing to the spirit, but many have been operating from the soul realm, run by their soul. Their thought was to get themselves satisfied through the soul. The satisfactions of the soul will never substitute for the satisfaction of the spirit, so give permission to be here and be moved by Heaven. We must give ourselves permission. We must say with the intent of our will:

I will go where I am led. I will go where I am directed. I will flow in His river. I will seek His presence.

Do you see these phrases? The Father said, "I will direct your spirit man as if one is giving oneself permission to forsake all else—all other things to get what the spirit needs."

The Father has heard the cry of His people all over the earth and His business is to answer.

We suddenly saw wings like we might imagine an angel to wear. Heaven informed us that these were the manifestations of the Father's winds. These were the representation of His winds—a visual image of the Father's winds, the way the winds are being released to the people's realms. The winds are a type of being. They will help have influence for how people are perceiving who they are, where they are in history, and how they can commune with the Father.

So many doctrines of demons exist that the people of the planet have fallen under, bringing trauma through bad teaching and the soul's hunt for solutions. But a straightening of the crooked path is coming back to planet earth. It *will* take place. He is God and God alone, there is no greater. There is none greater than the I AM. Things are changing.

A religious robe is going to fall off God's people. It already has begun slipping, and it is going to come off. The language about this will be some of the last two shifts. People will not know how to talk about this new move of God because of their inability to discern and put language around it. Some will try to capture it, but this is human nature. This is going to be hard to capture. It is simply going to be the work of God in His people. Where religion has made rules and regulations to capture God's people, an ease is coming to the true church. He loves her. He loves this church that He died for. He loves her heart. He loves her hands. He loves her voices. He loves her before she loved Him.

Lydia assured us that what we had released is seed, and remember—a seed takes time to grow, but it does grow. It does grow.

———·———

Chapter 6
Erecting Shields and Governing Realms

One morning, we engaged Heaven and checked in with Ezekiel, the ministry angel, and asked Ezekiel what he was doing. He replied, "We are busy working on the shields. The shields are up. *Tell the people to commission their angels to engage the shields that we are erecting.* Tell them to co-labor with us to engage both these shields *and* their own shields. We are building shields around the ministry. You are to commission your personal angels to work with me to engage the shields."

Ezekiel explained that his ranks are the shields—they form the shields. Shields let in things that we want in, so they let in the things of God, and they keep out the things of the enemy. Sometimes we feel bombarded, but there is nothing going on in the physical realm. This is what it may feel like to us when the shields that angels are forming are being set up, when they are acting on our behalf and they need our backup, and we need their backup. We need to work together, he explained, so commission our angels to work with the shields—the shield function of the ministry.

Governing Our Realm

Many humans have not understood their realms, and therefore, they have not understood that they have the right to *govern their realm*. Part of the governing of one's realm is to establish shields of protection. This is the work of angels. Many have seen the need for protection, but few have understood that the shields also work to allow in the blessings of God, the harmony of Heaven, the love of God, the associations He wants for us, the handshakes, and the agreements of people that the Father wants us to have so we all can agree.

We have realms and we are called to govern our realms.

All three realms that are in a person's being are to be governed.

There are other realms within our realm that intersect. For instance, we intersect the LifeSpring realm and so our realm is working with that realm. Therefore, we are helping to govern that realm.

We can flow to any of those realms, and we want to govern them with the help of angels, so govern them by:

- agreeing with God,

- agreeing with what He is doing,
- agreeing with his timeline,
- agreeing with His blessing, and
- commissioning our angels to make trades out of our realms to allow in what the Father is speaking about us, and to keep out what he is not speaking about,
- asking our angels to see to the shields regarding these things.

What strengthens a shield is:

- worship of God,
- intentional alignment with His Word spoken and verbalized,
- releasing of angels,
- the request to the Father for angels,
- the request of things for angels (like elixir and weaponry), and
- the belief in them that He has given them, He has made them for co-laboring, and he has given them to us for our good and that we collaborate with them and can collaborate with them well; that they do their job.

Vocalizing all of this is helpful to these angels who work to keep shields in place.

---

*By vocalizing these things aloud,
we help establish them in
the atmosphere about us.*

I am talking about a person right now—a three-part person: spirit, soul, and body. If we are talking about the spirit of that person, that spirit has a realm. That person's spirit must govern their realm and they do so with:

- spiritual truth,
- spiritual belief,
- spiritual faith,
- spiritual sight,
- spiritual activity.

Remember that the realms intersect and overlap; they both intersect and form the innermost part (our spirit) to our soul to our body realm—the container for the spirit and soul. Our realm trades with other realms. The intent of our realm is to trade with other realms who have righteous trades to trade with us so we can trade with them.

Ezekiel reminded us of a recent scenario involving a man named Tom. Tom had a trade with us of which we were aware. Tom was trying to expand the trade and we were not in agreement with the trade that he was wanting to expand. We had a problem with it. Ezekiel explained to us that what had happened is his trading with us had been misaligned. He had a previous trade with us, but when he made it, the *new* trade was outside of the previous trade he had made. We were not willing to make the new trade, and, because we were not willing to make that trade, the intersection of the realms could not happen.

What was happening was we were putting up or we were enforcing our shield against the trade, but the transaction could not have a resolution until we heard back from his sphere in his realm. We believed that it was an unrighteous trade that he was trying to make—not because it was bad, but because it is outside of the boundaries of the original trade. Therefore, we were not receiving the new trade into our realm. The agreement did not feel balanced to us.

Ezekiel explained, "One is asked to give more than one is willing to give. That is a definition of being stolen from." In this scenario, there was a dissonance between the realms. What exacerbated this dissonance was the lack of communication of what we were willing and not willing to trade. "When you communicate to him where you stand—what you are not willing to trade—then his realm will either align or retreat. If he retreats, that is not negative. Do not put that in a good or bad category. It is a neutral category. Retreat means he is gone—he is retreating to think about it. He will either agree or he will retreat. If he retreats, he may come back with another thing or he may just take time to agree." Ezekiel finished the illustration by reminding us of Amos 3:3,

How shall two walk together, lest they agree.

The Shields

We want to commission our angels to work with what is meant to come through to our realms because some things are meant to come through our shield. How will we know what is meant to come through our shield? They will have been written into books of Heaven about us.

Commission our angels to allow into our realm:

- the things that are written in Heaven about us
- the words of the Father,
- the books written about us in Heaven
- the maps about us in Heaven,
- the potentials about us in Heaven.

We want these things in the measured flow of Heaven to our realms.

We have a role in this to collaborate with the angels to accommodate the trades with Heaven, people, structures, etc.

Declaration for Erecting Shields & Governing Realms

I am a realm. I choose to govern my spirit realm in the name of Jesus through the love of God for me through my salvation—through my redemption in Christ Jesus, I govern my realm by agreement with God, agreement with what He is doing, agreement with his timeline, agreement with His blessing, and I commission my angels to make trades out of my realms to allow in what the Father is speaking about me, and to keep out what he is not speaking about me. I commission my angels to see to the shields regarding these things. I choose to govern my realms with the help of angels, by agreement with God: agreement with what He is doing, agreement with his timeline, and agreement with His blessing.

I also choose to govern my soul realm that it may grow and learn via my spirit the things of Heaven so that my mind is renewed in the ways of the Kingdom of God. I choose to feed my spirit only that which is beneficial. I also choose to govern my body realm that it be a healthy carrier of my spirit and soul realms and that I be able to glorify God in my body.

I commission my spirit to govern my realm with spiritual truth, spiritual belief, spiritual faith, spiritual sight, and spiritual activity.

I commission my angels to allow into my realm the things that are written in Heaven about me; the words of the Father, the books written about me in Heaven, the maps about me in Heaven, and the potentials about me in Heaven.

I want these things in the measured flow of Heaven to my realms.

I choose to collaborate with the angels to accommodate the trades Heaven desires: trades with Heaven, with people, with structures, etc.

I commission my personal angels to erect my personal shields.

I commission my angels to engage the shields that are to be erected by Heaven for my life.

I commission my angels to work with Ezekiel, his commanders, and his ranks regarding the shields they have erected and to work with the shield function of LifeSpring International Ministries.

I commission my angels to work with what is meant to come through these shields according to my book.

I commission my angels to make trades out of my realms to allow in what the Father is speaking about me and to keep out what He is not speaking about me.

I commission my angels to see to the shields regarding these things.

I commission my angels to collaborate with the angels assigned to LifeSpring International Ministries to develop the shield all around my spirit realm, to strengthen it, to support it, to engage it, to keep it activated, and to see to it.

I commission my angels to allow in the blessings of God, the harmony of Heaven, the love of God, the associations He wants for me, the handshakes, and the agreements of people that the Father wants for me so we can all agree with the purposes and desire of God.

I also commission my angels to help me understand where a breach has happened in a shield so that I can collaborate with the angels to strengthen the shield.

I choose to strengthen my shield by the worship of God, by intentional alignment with His Word spoken and verbalized, by the releasing of angels, by request of the Father for angels, by the request of things for angels (like elixir and weaponry), and by my belief in them, and that He has given them and made them for co-laboring, and he has given them to me for my good. I choose to collaborate with them, so they do their job.

I declare these things in the name of Jesus Christ.

Chapter 7

It is Time for Joy

Now is the time for the joy, joy, joy of the Lord to come to God's people. Many of God's children have been waylaid in their heartfelt worship of the Father. Ezekiel directed, "Remind the people to open the portal with praise, praise, praise! I will stir up praise. The Father can help you stir up your praise." We only need to ask for His help. Ask of the Father that we would be able to praise him in spirit and truth and that we would open our mouth. If we will determine in our heart with our will that we desire to praise God, He will assist us with His own praise.

Why is this? Because he knows His own worth and when we know His worth, we begin to see our own worth. It is time for the children of God to see their own worth.

How will we see this? By releasing the praise and worship to the Son and the Father. Holy Spirit is present to assist because He agrees with this truth. He agrees that we reflect the Father in the earth realm. He agrees with humankind. It is time to step into pools of grace, joy, and love.

The rotating seasons are created by the Father on purpose and with great intent to draw us forward in the cycle of our lives. This cycle is to draw us forward from joy to joy or another way to say that is from glory to glory. There is a great combination between rejoicing and His Glory. Some children of God feel bowed down, bowed over. Why are they bowed down? They are bowed over with anxiety, worry, trepidation, and fear. These resonant frequencies are not for God's people. How do we shed the garments of these frequencies that have clothed God's people? How are we to be free? We are to lift our eyes to seek after His kingdom, to combine voice and belief with the *verbal release* of God's praise. Atmospheres will shift because portals will open.

We can simply ask ourselves this question: If we feel full of anxiety, full of worry, full of trepidation and full of fear—if any of these evil frequencies are buffeting us, we can ask ourselves a question. "When was the last time I surrendered to His praise—not out of religious ritual, but out of the place in my heart that knows He is God?"

Some people try to start too big in their praise when they should just look inward and ask themselves a simple question, "What is the first thing I can thank him for? What is the first thing I can give him honor for?" Because the Father accomplished something. He has done something for us.

The review of these things from within our heart begins the roll call of praise and if we will do this verbally, what we will find is those who will speak in tongues will begin shortly to speak in tongues. But first start in English (or whatever our native language is), and then allow the bubbling up of that which dwells within us to come out.

Heaven is giving us a clue: Review the reasons we would honor God and from that review, release our thanksgiving—release our praise. Then ask Holy Spirit to pray through us in tongues and do not skimp but look within to give Him the rich sacrifice of praise.

If we feel so burdened that we cannot praise God, then it simply means that we have gone too long without looking to who He truly is. If we need the written Word of God, open the scriptures and read aloud the praise found therein. From this, allow our own spirit to begin to praise Him. This makes all the difference.

The angels are assigned to recognize the praise of humankind and to bring about the widening of portals. This widening of the portal in our realm to God's realm results in our sense of the nearness of His presence, His goodness, and His kindness. This draws our spirit forward even more. It works in tandem, but it must begin somewhere.

What is the beginning? It is the will's initiation of the desire whether to see an open portal open even wider, or to be rid of the burden of anxiety and fear. Use whatever motivates us, but do it and let it have its effect because it is effective every time.

If our spirit feels dry, engage in the verbal praise of God. If we feel far from God, engage in the verbal praise of God. I want to emphasize that the widening of the portal of the Spirit of God that gives us access to His presence cannot be achieved through the soul's ritual religious activity. That ritual activity will make our spirit feel drier.

How can we circumvent that? Many have been taught habits of religious ritual and they mistakenly think that this is their avenue of true worship. It is not. It is much simpler for a child of God to look inward to his heart and find the one thing that is most meaningful in his life, where God has touched him, where He has moved, or where He has shown Himself strong, and begin from that point. It is the inward heart of the man that recognizes God's touch there and blows on that ember within his heart until, with praise and worship, it is a flaming fire. That flaming fire will become a wildfire and the spirit of the man will soon become rich, watered, oiled, blessed, increased, and perceptive to his right of inheritance in spiritual places.

I want to encourage the people of God to throw off the burdens of anxiety for now is not the time to wear these garments of fear, anxiety, worry, and trepidation. The Father has not placed these on His people. Why do we wear them? It is because we simply have not understood the way to disrobe.

The Word of the Day is Encouragement

Now is the season for the rising of the sons and daughters in praise and worship from their heart, accepting the Father's love, His portion, and His care into their lives. Even burdens of prayer have seasons—types of prayer have seasons. A connection exists with cycles and seasons right now. Heaven is urging us to determine with our will:

- our release of love,
- our verbal release of praise,
- our verbal release of honor, and
- our verbal release of respect to who He is in order for that richness to begin to flow into us.

When verbally released, this is far greater than what we have ever released. When we release a little bit, we get a lot. Our spirit becomes buoyant—not only buoyant as floating in the river of God, but buoyant to catch the winds of God, and this is the time for new winds coming into the earth and these winds of God carry us forward even in our lives.

It is time to wash our face. It is time to determine that we will look to the horizon. It is time to determine that we are not tied to our past, especially to the negativity, anxieties, and worries that lie in our past. God has done a great work to dawn His hope within our heart.

How do we receive this? We begin with the honest internal review of our belief system, and we make the determination—the willful choice—to praise Him for what He has done and what truth we know there.

I am telling a spiritual mystery. The more we begin this verbal release of love, honor, respect, and praise, the wider the portal gets and the better we feel. I am talking about our soul because our soul has finally given way to our spirit and allowed our spirit to ascend to the richness of His Heavens, to the glory of His realms. From there, we will begin to freshly walk as a Kingdom citizen who has a body in the physical realm.

---

*Encouragement
is the word of the day.*

It is true for our oneness with the Father to rise from within our heart. We must know His truth about who we are and about who He is. Understand that one of the goals of Heaven is to develop the joy of the Lord in God's people because they feel and know His love, because they have *understood their access* to feel and know His love, and they have recognized that fear is a dissonant frequency the Father wants to be eradicated from their realms.

We often speak of imagination. What does imagination work for us? By imagining a people group who, in the face of the worst news—the most devastating anti-God scenarios being promoted and played out—imagine a people of God who, *nevertheless*, their primary come from is joy. Their primary come from is confidence that God is working on their behalf. Their primary come from is the sweetness of His presence that is like an aroma in their atmosphere all day long from the time they meet with Him at the break of day or in the morning.

Let *that* scenario float through our imagination because this is one way that the world is going to recognize that we belong to Jesus. It is our confidence, our peace, and our joy. It is the fact that we can love and have hope in the presence of what the enemy is doing, as he is building structures around us for evil and for his own dominion.

A seed of joy resides within God's people that even Satan cannot take.

That seed is the indwelling of Holy Spirit. It has been given as a gift through the resurrection of Christ. Water that seed.

Often, we are being funneled so we would behave and think a certain way, but God's people—no matter if they are being funneled by world structures to think and behave a certain way—they have within them the capacity (amid being funneled) to think and behave a certain way—being totally different. This shining[3] is the lamp of God within us. He wants to pour out more oil into our lamp so that our resident resonant frequency is the tool that he uses to attract many to notice not us

---

[3] Isaiah 60:1 – Arise, shine, for your light has come….

necessarily, but His Glory in us. Remember, this happens as we have surrendered to be who He is making us to be. It comes from surrender and acceptance of His perfection and His plan for us. Heaven wants to remind us that this is the benefit of being known as a son and daughter of God; remember to count His benefits in our lives.

Surrendering Burdens

The other thing is—when we find it difficult to look within our heart and find the one thing that we can begin to thank the Father for and to worship Him for in the quiet stillness of our alone time with Him, if we find this difficult, there is a good chance that one of our realms is not at peace. If it is our body realm not at peace, it may simply be the need for restorative sleep, and that request of the Father will be answered.

If it is our soul that is not at peace, our soul has determined to carry a burden it is not meant to carry and has not surrendered.

The surrender of burdens is just that: surrendering from the soul and determining that God will help us from our spirit and in speaking to our soul to lay down this burden and not pick it up because Jesus is able to help us from His Kingdom realm.

If we are weary in our body, physical rest is needed. Physical rest is helpful. How plain does Heaven have to be? Go to bed earlier, take a nap, get up later where we can catch up our physical rest. Do not apologize for the need of this physical rest. We are a three-part being and all parts of us interact.

Some do not know how to speak to their soul. It is possible to speak to one's soul and say, "It is time to rest. I speak to you and say, rest. I speak to you and say, 'we are surrendering these anxieties, we are surrendering these burdens, we are not carrying them. We are laying them down. We are leaving them behind and we are surrendering them to the Father in whom all things begin and end, and to Jesus who has Lordship over our lives.'"

Sometimes a release of an old habit is exactly the answer we are looking for. Sometimes our habits have made us have some routine in our lives and therefore the joy of the Lord has trouble being seeded there. Therefore, the surrendering of some habits is helpful so that we regain a resilience out of the new thing God wants to create within us. Simply ask the Father, "Is there a habit in my life I am connected to that would be better for me to surrender and allow a new formation of something?"

If this is the case, ask for help from Holy Spirit. "I ask for help from angels to lay the habit down and receive as a gift something new in its place." This keeps the spirit of man buoyant and flexible and keeps the soul from becoming like concrete.

Many people do not know that what they are looking for is the new because they are so preoccupied with the past that they have not surrendered. What their heart and their spirit is crying out for is the experience of the new. Give ourselves verbal permission to receive the new that the Father, who is always creating, wants to bring into our lives. Not only does this bring joy, but it also brings hope as well. Ask the Father for the new that He wants to bring and form within us.

———·———

Chapter 8
Utilizing Keys

We were wondering how to teach the people to receive what had just been bestowed from Heaven, which was regarding keys. Heaven explained that a key is for unlocking. Keys are symbols of unexplored territories or spaces. This can equate to a gifting, an expansion within our realm—many things. A key from Heaven unlocks a new place we have yet to explore. Heaven is not talking about geographical spaces, but dimensional spaces. A new key provides access. It could be access to a new manner of living our lives, a new relationship, a new gifting, or a new manner of being. Remember, God is the great I AM and some of these keys are to our 'I AM-ness' as He expands himself in us.

The Father is delivering many keys right now, and he has sent angels with keys and key rings into the earth to dimensional places in His people with the enlarged understanding of spiritual realms. We need keys to access what we have not yet had access to. I am not talking about places in the heavenly realm. We already have access there and can freely move in the heavenly realms. These are tangible and intangible things in our world. In the 3-D world, they will manifest as tangible things, but in the spirit world they will be apprehended, walked through, or walked into—that is a better way to say it, walked into—in tangible ways.

For instance, wealth from the kingdom of God will *manifest in the heart* of the believer who has unlocked that area, having been given a key to unlock that area in his heart that he may begin moving in new paradigms of all manner of wealth. I am not talking about money. I am talking about wealth or riches. Some keys unlock riches which equates to financial increase. This could also be financial increase, not in money, but in objects like houses, cars, real estate, buildings, travel, and associations. Some have been given keys to new giftings. These are spiritual giftings that touch the church—the gathered ecclesia, the corporate bride, or the corporate body. They make her glorious when engaged in corporate things. Some are receiving keys of knowledge. This is like access to realms of books, libraries of books, the mind of Christ, or the knowledge of the Father. Some are being given keys of relationships that have now been unlocked. Some are keys to destiny scrolls because now is the time for their unlocking. This has to do with mountains and access to mountains. Some have been given keys to illumination like the place of His flame and flame within us—a new dimensional access for his power to come through us. Keys level us up by giving us access to places we have not explored or had access to yet.

Utilizing a Spiritual Key

The way one utilizes a spiritual key is to receive it with joy, agree with its work of unlocking what has previously been closed, and then take the key and insert it into a spiritual lock, like a door in the spirit. (That would be like a prophetic act.) Put the key in the lock, turn the key, and open the door.

A key holder has <u>already</u> been given the authority to open the door.

The key had to come first. The door has always been there. The person may have stood in front of the door for a while spiritually speaking, but once given the key, they put the key in the lock and they turn the key, but then they must grasp the handle of the door and open it. This type of door swings inward. It swings into the space that we are accessing and provides our entrance to explore the space.

Dropped Keys

In past seasons there have been dropped keys. We may find these dropped keys when we are traversing the realms of Heaven. We may find these dropped keys in physical territories of the 3-D realm. When we find a key, ask the Lord if this is my key or if we have a right to use it. If we do, we will be told what it opens. If we do not, we have recovered it for the Kingdom and an angel will come to receive it back to His Kingdom. We have redeemed a key. This is recorded in Heaven about the individual receiving a key.

Exploring What Has Been Unlocked

To intentionally explore what has been unlocked is a journey with the Holy Spirit and angels. We can know the pleasure the Father has in seeing us engage what He has released the key to unlock.

Humans cannot achieve this on the fly. This takes willful and intentional spiritual work to be a child, to step into the realms of Heaven, and to ask about the key—ask to be informed. Write it down. Follow it through in the natural realm and let it build out as it grows.

Keys are tied to the times. Keys are always tied to times and seasons, to time cycles, ages, and forward movement because the Kingdom of God *is* being built on earth as it is in Heaven.

———·———

Chapter 9

Reverse Covenants Within Contracts

We recently experienced a situation with someone that seemed to turn to offense quickly. It did not seem logical to us, but in the process, Heaven unveiled some things to us that are helpful. This information will benefit you as well.

Sometimes when people donate to our ministry, they have an ulterior motive behind their giving. Rather than simply creating a godly trading floor that can bless their lives, they have an expectation that is not healthy. If the person making the donation has a history of manipulation and control, they may find themselves doing things out of wrong motivations. This can happen when people feel that, because they have given to a ministry, they then have the right or authority to direct what that ministry does. For some (without their knowledge) they are operating out of the knowledge of the Tree of Good and Evil to control trades they make. A veil was pulled back allowing us to see what was occurring with this individual. It was as if the tentacles of an octopus were seeking to reach into various aspects of the ministry.

We were warned to watch and see if these tentacles grew. They represented the propensity for control through what one sows into. If we saw it grow, we were invited to allow Ezekiel to take care of it which he would be happy to do.

We did not want it to grow, so we asked if we could engage it now. Heaven explained to us that this was like a reverse covenant within contract which says, "If I sow into you, then I can control you." It is deeply religious, and it is from a manipulation-based spirit and an offshoot of the Jezebel spirit.

We were not interested in dealing with it further—not merely for our benefit, but for the benefit of the donor in question. We did not want them to be controlled by it either. Lydia instructed us to take it to the Court of Cancellations.

Explaining what we had seen, we were told that it was a threat of manipulation and a threat that comes from the spirit of manipulation and control. It is using our trade to reverse engineer a covenant within contract. It says, "If I trade with you, I therefore have the right to manipulate you."

Covenants within Contracts result from ungodly trades. For example, you take your car to be serviced at a local garage. Unknown to you, the owner or manager has made an illegal trade with darkness to procure more business. He has agreed, in exchange for an increase in business, for his customers to be taxed by the enemy due to their trade with that garage.

The customer gets the repair done, but shortly afterward, they need another repair and return to the same garage for the work to be accomplished. This continues in a cycle. The customer has been affected by a covenant (with darkness) within the contract—the original agreement to simply repair the original issue.

These covenants within contracts can come in many forms. One needs to access the Court of Cancellations for any covenants within contracts to be cancelled and all taxation to cease. Then access the Court of Reclamations to request a return of all things lost to us because of the garage owner/manager's ungodly deed.

Court of Cancellations

We immediately requested Lydia's assistance as we accessed the Court of Cancellations to get this issue taken care of.

> *We request access to the Court of Cancellations. We are here concerning the reverse engineering of a covenant within contract that says, "If I sow into you, I can control you."*

The participant with this has sown into the ministry. We request the cancellation of this reverse-engineered contract with this person and its tentacles into the ministry, so those things are removed and separated entirely from the ministry, in Jesus' name.

We request warrior angels for the defeat of this. The spirit of Jezebel had made an inroad to this ministry through this human. We petition this court for warrior angels to accomplish a cutting off every gained dimensional access, every inroad, and every unseen evil seed.

We request Your Honor, that this be done through warrior angels on behalf of LifeSpring International Ministries.

We also ask an amendment on behalf of the human involved in this that they be provided with insight, revelation, and understanding regarding the religious ritual of sowing that they have been deceived into believing a measure of manipulation is their right. We forgive this person, and we bless them, and we release them in Jesus' name.

Father, we forgive this person because they know not what they do, being under deception through religious rituals. We ask You to forgive them through the blood of Jesus. It is our great honor to forgive them and release them from their guilt, in Jesus' name.

We saw paperwork being given to the warrior angels and we began thanking the Father for the scroll being written for the donor. We saw the scroll of the Father's love being delivered to the person.

> *Father, we praise You that the spirit of Jezebel has been chastened, cut off, and caused to flee by Your power. We praise You Jesus that Your Kingdom will expand.*

We then went to the Court of Reclamation.

> *Father, we ask permission to enter the Court of Reclamation in Jesus' name, having come from the Court of Cancellations regarding a court case. We step into this court to request counsel of the court. What may we request as a restitution?*

> *We request, in Jesus' name, a seven-fold expansion of LifeSpring International Ministries according to the Kingdom of God and the will of the Father and we receive this.[4]*

> *We enter this petition into this court, but we receive the verdict as an authentic backlash and weapon against the spirit of Jezebel and against the deceiver in Jesus' name.*

Scrolls and maps then began coming into the courtroom regarding our petition.

---

[4] That is what we heard to request from the Court of Reclamations.

The information about the reverse-engineering of a covenant within contract can be extremely helpful to ministry leaders and business owners or managers too. Sometimes customers will make a small trade but expect to have all the privileges the best customers or contributors are entitled to.

The degree of investment always equates to a degree of engagement.

The greater the investment, the greater the degree of engagement one can expect.

Many companies operate this way because it honors those who have chosen to trade with them regularly. Our ministry practices this principle of honor with our membership program. Our Platinum Members have the greatest amount of engagement with us because they have the greatest level of investment and trade with us.

Ministry leaders often experience the subtle (and sometimes not so subtle) attempts to coerce a ministry to do certain things because they want to see a certain result. Giving to a ministry in order for one to control that ministry is wicked. If we have been guilty in the past, we should repent and make restitution to those affected if we can.

> *To publicly revile someone and then merely privately repent to them is not always appropriate nor does it represent true repentance.*

For example, several years ago, a ministry leader rebuked me publicly for something he perceived I had done. I was not guilty of the alleged crime, but facts were not important to him at the time. Years later, he came to apologize privately to me for what he had done. I accepted his apology and had forgiven him long ago, but a private apology for a public rebuke may not be a sincere apology. If we were bold enough to rebuke publicly, we should be bold enough to apologize publicly.

Ministry leaders who have experienced attempts at control by donors may want to go to the courts (Court of Cancellations and Court of Reclamations) as were described above and get these things rectified so they and their ministry can move forward. Leaders, simply be aware that we must walk in forgiveness, regardless of the actions or the outcomes. Let us walk as sons of the Most High God.

Chapter 10
Relationships & Trades

The subject was crossovers. Crossovers are where something outside our lives tries to come into our lives, or vice versa relating to (in this case) the ministry. We had been discussing this with Ezekiel, our chief ministry angel. He explained that crossovers were trying to happen and we needed to know a few things about them. Crossovers are neutral and where there is no agreement, trades do not happen.

Because we have put up a shield around the ministry and we have commissioned Ezekiel, his commanders, and his ranks with receiving the things from the Father that are good for the ministry, but keeping out the things that are not, crossovers play out differently in different ways, depending upon the manner of trade in which the person approaches us.

Lydia joined the conversation regarding a relationship that had been breached some months before. Lydia's first instruction was to be sure that any woundedness from this person's activity had been healed because a wounded place is a place for a fear to crash—a hidden fear to crash.

We took her advice, searched our hearts, and admitted that we still hung onto a small degree of woundedness from the situation. We asked the Father to heal us of the woundedness in Jesus' name. We surrendered the place to Jesus and thanked Him for His healing work. We invited the peace of God into that place and received Heaven's touch in our realms.

Understanding Crossovers

Ezekiel spoke up, "This topic is about trade. It is also about building. It is also about navigation and finding the true path." Remember, we can walk with the Spirit of Wisdom.

The field in which we are sowing has many seeds and yet the harvest of the seeds is still forthcoming. They are growing but they are not at harvest stage. We are also amid some crossovers. Some of our leaders were branching out and doing other things within the ministry. These acts are trades through the field of the ministry. We have many crossovers.

At its simplest form, different people in the ministry were doing different things. They were crossing over. Where they have been trading in one form, now they were trading in a new or additional fashion. Within the sphere of the LifeSpring's realm, we could see what looked like new connections or new bridges, but they were really links and not bridges. The different people were linking out and, by linking out, the ministry was expanding. Because of this expansion, we had those who were trying to cross into our realm.

Lydia told us that we had to determine if we would have a trade or not. Remember to think in terms of the neutrality of trade. Until an agreement is made, it is neutral. We typically think in terms of bad or good, but know that some things are neutral. We must give ourselves permission to have a neutrality of thought about someone reaching out to us and it is just that—it is a neutral place to watch and oversee. Over time, we will obtain direction about what to do about the neutrality in which we hold them—whether to reach out or to retreat.

A trade is made by agreement from both parties. When the agreement feels righteous and when the agreement feels balanced, the trade is made. If not, it can be held in a status of neutrality. The belief system of the heart wants to divide it into positive or negative, but there is a space for neutrality in this situation and holding this neutrality will be necessary.

Heaven advised us to hold this person in a neutral place. Sometimes that is not the answer we want or even the answer we thought we were going to get, but it *is* the answer for some situations. We had to make room for a space called the place of neutrality.

We were told to realize that things want to play on the trade. Fear wants to play on the trade. Fear wants to have a say. Fear wants to shape the trade. Other things want to shape the trade, such as expectations or memories. All these play on the trade.

For our clarification, Ezekiel repeated what Lydia said about holding something in a neutral place.

> *Sometimes we need to hold these things in a neutral place until a moment of time comes where we have a new thought.*

As watchmen, we have a new thought. We have a decision. We have our own boundaries. Another thing that can play on a trade is fear; fear can play on a trade and boundaries can play on a trade. These boundaries are God-given. They are the safety net. They provide the safety rails.

In this situation, we did not feel that a trade was eminent, because we felt a boundary line since our boundary lines at this time did not include what this person was offering to trade. Boundaries are moveable, but they are not static in that they can grow with the maturity of the person. They can grow with the calling. They can grow with the realization of a new scroll. They morph. They can change.

> *What we want is the Godhead setting the boundaries for us.*

We do not want our soul realm changing the boundaries or moving the markers, because the soul realm will do that out of manipulation, control, and a seeking for power and illegal authority. As we see it come near, we can hold it in a place of neutrality until we determine where our boundaries are as given by the Father, and what has changed in those boundaries as related to new scrolls that may or may not have come.

Do not forget, our human will is also involved in this too. We do have choice, and the Father honors the human will and it is okay if the human will has decided how to respond to the trade. The downfall of this is where the human will is making the decisions *out of the woundedness* that is still in one's belief system or in their heart that is not completely whole. That would be an area to surrender to the Lord so that wholeness comes to that place, in order for better willful decisions to be made.

For instance, with this person, we felt like we could walk with them in this way, but we did not feel an ease to walk with them in another way. That is good to notice. Often, some things exist in life where even Heaven is not going to give us the immediate direction, because all things are working together for good. Simply continue to watch, see, and understand. Therefore, walking with wisdom is needed. We will begin to gain perspective about it. We could simply say we are in a place of gaining perspective about this. We are going to wait for God's perspective on this.

One of the principles of life is that some people add to our lives while others take away. Sometimes we will have people in our lives for a season and they add to our lives, yet at the end of that season, allow the relationship to take on the form it needs to take. Do not hold tightly to relationships whose time to end has come. We can part amicably, simply understanding that we both have deposited into the other's life what we were meant to deposit.

Also, sometimes our soul longs for a relationship that Heaven knows is not healthy for us to have. Allow Heaven to build our relationships according to our scrolls. Do not try to build what God is not wanting built in our lives. It will only bring misery. Allow Heaven to build our lives. Heaven always knows best.

Refrigerator Rights

Another way to look at relationships like this is how, in our lives, some people have refrigerator rights. We have some people in our lives that, when they come to our home, we do not mind if they make themselves at home and go to the refrigerator themselves to get something to drink or to get a snack. However, not everyone entering our home has the same level of access to our refrigerator. The yard guy coming to our home does not have refrigerator rights. However, our best friend who we have known for years does.

Another aspect is to not assume we have rights we may not have with an individual or ministry.

Relationships must be built, and the building of relationships usually takes time. It would be dishonoring to someone to assume refrigerator rights that are not actually bestowed. To assume rights that do not exist may cause a delay in the actual bestowal of those rights. In some cases, these wrong assumptions can cause an abortion of the rights that Heaven may have intended.

Some people have had refrigerator rights with us in the past, but when the relationship is abruptly ended, getting those refrigerator rights restored may not be a quick process. Choose wisely those in our lives who should have refrigerator rights and those who should not; our lives will be simpler and safer for it.

———·———

Chapter 11
The Discipline of Our Soul

As we engaged Heaven one day, we requested to meet with Lydia, our ministry advisor. Although she did not initially appear, a substance appeared in the spirit that was purple in color. No explanation came concerning this, but now we could hear Lydia instructing us to understand that we are both kings and priests in His Kingdom. Nevertheless, He (the Father) is the King. Even children must be made to understand that the King is who He is, out of the selection of who He has been made to be—and if Jesus is King of His Glory, then we are kings and priests in His Kingdom and we are learning to walk in authority as a king and in ministry to our God as a priest. Kingly conduct becomes us. Kingly conduct is related to honor and respect for the position of the King.

Some have never seen themselves in their own authority. Some see themselves as the dirt under the King's feet. Others see themselves as unnoticed in His sight, alone and without recourse. None of these things are the way to view oneself. Nevertheless, these are the lenses that are being used day-to-day by various people. Some have been taught as a young child that they had no value. Others, through the experience of always being caught in a whirlwind, have grasped at straws so often that the grasping is what they do instead of settling to hear and settling to receive. The use of quietening[5] at the hands of angels would be helpful for people like this and for their atmospheres. These people are so busy trying to 'figure it out' that they ceased *receiving* the answers a while ago.

An Everyday Choice

It is true that in our walk with the Lord, we will choose *every day* to follow Him. We will choose to set our mind aside and set our heart on Him so that the Spirit of the Lord can speak to us. As we have learned, our soul wants domination over our spirit, and we are slowly learning ways of increasing the time our spirit is forward as we are living from our spirit. We are learning to rest by the *practice* of being spiritual. However, if we are being soulish and thinking we are being spiritual, we are self-deceived.

Practicing quiet moments of hearing the voice of the Father, and of the Son, and of the Spirit is a good practice. Meditating on His Word is not meditating on *the* word. Meditating on *the* word leads one to strive and to try to

---

[5] Quietening is a tool that angels can use to settle the atmosphere of a situation.

figure out where one is in the world. Let me provide a clearer view of what I mean by meditating on His Word—it is meditation on what He has spoken to us individually. I am talking about the *rhema* conversation, not the *logos* written word. Other people's experiences, even Paul's experience, as it is written in the Bible, is not our own personal experience of this God who speaks to His own. We must hear Him for ourselves. We must be moved by Him. We must achieve this through surrender and following Him. This involves sacrificing time and learning a new way. Our mind has partaken of the Tree of the Knowledge of Good and Evil and our spirit has partaken of the Tree of Life, but which tree will give fruit in our being is what is working out.

More fruit in our being comes from the practice of being a spirit-led, spirit-forward person. Spiritual things, spiritual beings, spiritual understanding, and spiritual knowledge becomes more evident to our *spirit* man. I am not talking about the soul realm knowledge. I am not talking about the continual analysis of what *has* been written. I am talking about meditating on what we are hearing firsthand.

Many of God's children do not believe they can hear Him firsthand. Many have surrendered hearing Him firsthand to other people in their lives such as their spouse and those operating as prophets. Would we not say that the world is full of voices? But are we discerning *the* voice as well—the voice of His presence? He speaks through the voice of His presence. Our maturation is connected to the sacrifice of time to hear Him speak and to further the meditation that He has spoken to us. This results in spiritual growth.

It can plainly be said that if we want to grow up in Christ, we must develop our faith—our belief to hear Him personally. Notice that I did not say to hear Him answer our questions; I simply said to hear Him. What is He saying? What is on His mind? What has come to us from His heart? What does He want to give us? What does He want to show us? What does He want to bless us with? How high does He want to take us today?

Is the flow rapid or is it a languishing pool of refreshing? The people must hear the Lord for this is the access given through the King. The people must hear His counsel, His wisdom, and His knowledge. They must hear the voice of His might. They must hear the roar of His wind. They must hear the increase of His Glory, and most of all—they must be willing to let Him lead. Who oversees this train?

The purple we had seen earlier was a reminder of the royalty of our inheritance in Christ as a King and a Priest.[6] There are some who do not know it. There are some who do not know it because they have not paused to hear it. "What does the King want to do?" is one of the

---

[6] "But you are God's chosen treasure—priests who are kings, a spiritual "nation" set apart as God's devoted ones." 1 Peter 2:9 (TPT)

better questions we can ask. What is upon His mind to do?

I want to share something that might be clarifying. Even with that question, some will listen for the wrong answer. "What does the King have on His mind to do?" means that the King will share with us what is on His mind. He is not necessarily directing our every move from that question. *This* has been assigned to angels. They are in charge of directing us. They are in charge of playing out, or causing to be played out, many things that are written about this era, or about the nations, the families, the associations, and the groupings of God.

We gain our everyday sense of what is to be done from following the One who dwells within us, from He who freely tweaks us with a small, slight check in our spirit.

Many of us are receiving these checks of the Holy Spirit because this is Holy Spirit's work within us. The Holy Spirit will stop us from speaking. The Holy Spirit will stop us from making a particular choice. The Holy Spirit is not *difficult* to understand. He sounds like us sometimes, but He sounds like our *best* us. He is us indwelt from the Father, and He reflects what He sees. He sees and moves from the Father.

The Discipline of the Soul

Our work is the discipline of our soul in the obedience to the Spirit that dwells within us and speaks what He says. The central item of this is faith. We must believe that we hear God to hear Him. We must believe ourselves as a beloved one to feel loved. We must walk in the obedience of faith. The good news is that we can ask for *more* faith. We can even ask for God's faith. We can ask for faith to come and fill us, but it is also true the Father has given us the choice to believe.

What are we doing with our belief? What is our belief believing? Where is our belief leading us? What is our belief leading us to investigate? Have we paused to ask the Lord if this belief is His belief? This is what I mean by asking the King, "What is upon Your mind?"

There are many who are trying to get instantaneous answers to the 3-D physical realm. While we know God is concerned with what concerns us, have we paused as His child to find out what concerns Him? What is He concerned about? Are these not many good things to journal about and consider? There are many voices in the world today. Not all worldly voices are beneficial to be listened to or should be listened to. Pay attention to His spirit within, directing us, giving us unction regarding the questions that we have. It is the work of Holy Spirit in our inner man who is leading us, but we must tune into Him. We must allow His voice. We must agree with His closeness, His presence, His nearness.

The work of the Holy Spirit is to grow up the church, to change the individual and the corporate expression of who He is into a purer reflection of Heaven so that it will come to earth through His sons and daughters who are sensing Him.

The time for miracles is coming. It is truly a brief time before the miracles of God are going to be displacing other things. But while these miracles are timed and will begin to operate in the lives of people, the soul realm has a certain expectation of what a miracle is and is not. The *spirit* of the man knows the intensity of the miracle as it is being brought about even in secret. Whether a secret miracle or public...

A miracle is a movement of God that bends the laws of the physical realm to the will of the King.

Is this not for the children of that King to manifest? It most certainly is.

If we are patient in this process, with a high degree of faith and belief, never backing down from our belief, this will accomplish many miracles in the days ahead.

Miracles are brought on the winds of God and are directed by the Holy Spirit. Miracles come through mature sons of God.

There are many levels of miracles. Speaking in tongues is a miracle. Accessing heavenly realms is a miracle. Knowing the voice of the Father is a miracle. We have elementary miracles all around us.

We are learning to steward elementary miracles so that we can grow into stewarding the greater works of God.

The Commitment of the Angel

At this point, the angel Ezekiel began to speak. He told us that he was on assignment. He said that the angels who are loyal to the King and to the Father are committed in their loyalty to the expansion of His Glory. The angels assigned to people are committed to the expansion of God's Glory inside them, around them, and with them. The partnership of humankind with the angelic race is to bring about the manifestation of the Glory of God.

We cannot do this alone. We cannot manifest the Glory of God in the earth realm as it is today without the help of the angelic host. Angels have long looked forward to this day. The wisdom of the Father is exceedingly great, and the angels are aligned with His wisdom and counsel.

The angels that are with God are going to be with God forever. *There are no more turncoat[7] angels.* There were previously, but there are no more. Now it is time for humans to collaborate with the host of Heaven, to work with this glory force, who are 100% zealously committed to the expansion of His Glory in the earth. Humans are really going to have to get this! Angels of the Host of Heaven have more might than any pitiful turncoat could ever think of.

No wonder the resistance to collaborating with angels is so evident when the release of the partnership of mankind and angels is so powerful. It is powerful, and it is part of His Glory. Part of His Glory is His *wisdom* in this. Can we understand this?

---

*It is the wisdom of God
to cause humankind to operate
with the host of Heaven.*

It is the wisdom of God.

Can we rejoice in this? Can we believe in the wisdom of this great depth and in the release of the host of Heaven to collaborate with the men and women of earth?

---

[7] Definition of Turncoat: **One who traitorously switches allegiance.**

Our Arrangement with Angels

The Father's release of His arrangement to collaborate with the sons and daughters of God and the angelic—this is for the release of His Glory which equates to the release of His power and His might by spiritual means. It has always been this way. This is what the illegal trade of that power and might was all about—it was doing it without Him; it was circumventing God.

That is what the Tree of the Knowledge of Good and Evil was all about. If Satan could get humans to eat from that tree, then he could rule them, because he could make them afraid. He rules by fear. He *always* rules by fear. He will *always* rule by fear. He will never stop ruling by fear, and it is true what scripture says: the Father has *never* given humankind the spirit of fear.[8]

Let our faith be like Abraham. God is working out a good plan. Our faith is not in the plan, it is in the Creator of the plan, with the belief that He will show us the steps of His plan where it affects us.

All trauma, all fear, all wounds, all pain are simply present in our lives to divert us from this faith—to cause the frequencies in us and around us to resonate at a wrong frequency so that we are not receiving all that we need to receive from His authority, from His Name.

---

[8] 2 Timothy 1:7

> *We have a responsibility
> <u>not</u> to embrace fear.*

We have a responsibility to repent for fear where we have agreed with it. We also have a responsibility not to let the voice of fear teach us. The Father will never speak from a voice of fear.

Meditate on the voice of wisdom and counsel, the voice of goodness, the voice of truth, the voice of light, the voice of joy, the voice of victory. Ask ourselves, "What does the voice of victory say about this?" We know these answers; these are not withheld from us. They come from within us by His Spirit.

The Fivefold Gifting

God has placed in His house on earth the ministry of the fivefold gifting.

> *The fivefold gifting as it is being
> established in the earth is related
> to the government of the realm
> of the manifestation of His Glory.*

The leading of this fivefold into understanding, grasping the unseen power and might of God—the supernatural—is some of what will be released in future days. The future does contain this.

We suddenly saw an image of us in the front car of a roller coaster, already on the track. The tracks were very up and down, like on a wild ride, and we were in the very front. Ezekiel explained that the front car is for the risk takers. Those looking for the most excitement get in the first car. He explained that he was just showing us the role of going first. If no one demonstrates this to other people—at least to those who are being drawn by the Spirit to hear what we are releasing—if no one goes first, how will anybody go?

Most of us do not get in the first car on a roller coaster—at least not often. We usually have been in the middle cars a lot more.

Remember, the Father can bring good things out of all things. He can use it for our good so let Him use it.

———·———

Chapter 12
Collapsing Storms

Ezekiel seemed to emerge from between two whirlwinds or dust storms (or as some call them—dust devils). He had them under his hands as he walked through them. We watched as he lowered his hands and the storms got smaller. When he raised his hands, they got larger. We were going to need greater understanding about what he was showing us.

He explained that we were looking at a storm from a spiritual viewpoint. He was showing us how capable angels are at dealing with storms. He was showing us this because he had been putting out or flattening a few storms for the ministry.

"This is my work," Ezekiel explained. "I can collapse storms. I need help and partnership, but I collapse storms." We (the ministry) had a couple storms on our hands. We had a storm with one of our students and we had a storm with a client.

Ezekiel told us, "You have storms that the enemy brings as a type of weapon against you. It is a weapon in the form of a distraction. It is coming through a hardship in a person's life that the enemy is using against the work and the calling of this ministry."

LifeSpring International Ministries is called to lead the Body of Christ in understanding spiritual revelation.

Ezekiel, his commanders, and his ranks have the capacity to collapse realms. A storm can be a realm. A realm is a type of entity. It is sentient.[9] The realm called the storm is loosed upon people, timelines, businesses, and ministries *to bring forward movement to a halt.*

Many people see the detail of the storm without recognizing what the author of the storm is saying. Very few understand they can stop the storm like Jesus did from the boat.[10] Things are stirred by the enemy's plans. Remember that the enemy is evil, seeking to kill, destroy, or steal from a ministry or business operating in blessing and forward movement with growth. When a consistent growth pattern comes up before the enemy, it is a vile thing in his sight. Under the focus of demonic councils, he tries to stop it, and he tries to bring ruination or digression or a halt to their blessing and to their movement. The enemy trembles when the sons of God

---

[9] The capacity to be aware of sensations and feelings.
[10] Mark 4:35-41

increase and the sons of God are now increasing, and the enemy is terrified. This causes him to release a storm against these individuals or entities and the storm has what we would call an algorithm, and this gives the storm its so-called sentience.

We will need to commission angelic hosts to collapse the storm.

> *In the scripture, the storm came to deviate Jesus and the disciples from the mission at hand.*

That is one descriptive nuance of a storm: its purpose is to deviate us from where we are going. It wants to make us go around, make us slow down, or make us stop. If we have a storm, it has been stirred by evil thrones and evil trading routes and trade in that sort of activity.

Ezekiel stated, "I am going to show you how to commission angels in the Host of Heaven to collapse the realm called the storm. Kat Kerr uses different language. She looses the Armies of Heaven to *shred the activity* of the enemy—the activity of those involved in evil trade."

We asked, "How do we release the armies of Heaven?"

Ezekiel explained, "There are different classes of the race of angels assigned to these capacities. Some are more skilled than others. They know who they are. This *is* new to some in the church operating like this, but new is new.

As sons of God who are maturing in Jesus Christ, seeking to operate from Him by the Holy Spirit, we are given access to command armies—warring angels, the host of Heaven, the armies of God. In fact, these are based on our assignment and where we are in the season of life that we are in. There are various levels of our access to different armies. As a ministry, someone must direct the army that has been assigned to the ministry. Ezekiel had been doing this because we had commissioned him.

Ezekiel, the commanders, and the ranks form an army, but there are other angel armies that are not dedicated to specifically work with this ministry, though he has access to them.

At this point, Ezekiel suggested we trade with Mitchell. We requested that he join us, and we invited him to help us understand. Mitchell told us that some of what he was going to share with us—this ability has been reserved for these days. We must understand that not all the knowledge that is being released from the Father right now has always been on the planet or has been released to men in prior times. Some has been reserved for the days in which we are living. There is more knowledge in books that have been reserved for our future generations for the days in which they will walk, but now is the time for this knowledge to be shared with God's children through His sons. The storms that are stirred by demonic powers, thrones, principalities, and dominions are set against the people of God, and as

Ezekiel has told us, especially set against the expansion of the Kingdom.

> *The storm scene seeks to remove the ease with which we are completing a mission and an assignment.*

> *Please know that some of the things we call storms are not storms.*

Some of the things we call storms are simply the uphill climb to live among the world—those blinded by the Tree of the Knowledge of Good and Evil, those not eating of the right fruit, those seeking after other gods—even self-idolatry—and, in their deception, they end up building idols to themselves. Some of these idols that they have built are of themselves as they idolize themself.

Nevertheless, satanic activity comes against those who are breaking through to new levels of knowledge, power, and understanding. It comes against those who are taking possession of released seed, of harvested seed, and who are learning to build in the spirit realm as we are growing in relationship with the Father, and the Son, and the Holy Spirit.

> *A storm sent against us*
> *can primarily be discovered*
> *because it is very distracting.*

Our ability to collapse a storm comes at the hands of angels. If we have relationships with angels, we can see how helpful this is. If we have no relationship with angels or have never used them, we can see how it is necessary to begin relationship with the angels of God so that the partnership of children of men will grow into deeper understandings of one another.

Our personal angels know all the details of what we are doing. Even though we are not aware of him on a day-to-day basis, he is aware of us. How has this happened? It has happened over time. This is how relationships grow up, even our relationships with angels.

For a storm to collapse, we need to know that a storm is built on frequency.

> *The opposite frequency*
> *must be spoken to the storm.*

Jesus *spoke* peace to the storm, but he also *commanded* it to cease and desist. A son of God's authority plays into this. Our confident authority in who we are to speak to the storm is one thing. Our confident ability to speak to angels to help us settle the storm is another thing. We need to see and understand that there are various levels of understanding of our own confidence in who we are called to be in the spirit.

As we are operating spirit forward, spirit first, and as our spirit becomes aware of a storm, we can simply release angels to this activity. Here is how we do it: Always in the authority of the highest name in Heaven, we release and commission the angels of God to bring to nothing, to bring down out of the second heaven's atmospheres, all demonically run and instigated storms set against our path.

Evil storms are made of frequencies of darkness. Therefore, we release angelic armies—we release heavenly light. We can release the lightning of God, the light of God. Notice what we are doing. This has nothing to do with other human beings. This has everything to do with demons and those working in league with demons, especially those working in evil trade routes.

We can commission angels to bring the frequency of this storm to zero—to flatten it, to collapse it. We can even use the word collapse—to collapse its timeline in the name of Jesus. We use the name of Jesus because it is the authority of the highest name. Angels hearken to this.

We can ask input from Holy Spirit, but we can also ask our angel, "Am I involved in a storm?" If a storm has touched our sphere or our realm, we can commission angels to collapse the storm. In the earth realm we will see a storm collapsed when:

- the clouds fall apart,

- the wind stops the movement
- especially when the enlargement of the impending threat is dissolved and dissipates and comes to nothing.

Mitchell inquired, "Do we see all this language that I am using that can be used in our commissioning of the angels to collapse storms?"

"Oh, how the enemy does not want the sons of God to understand this tactic of his. Now, just like everything we teach you, some will run the gamut of using this technique too often and wear out their angels; they will wear out angel armies assigned to them. Some will hear of it and never use it, even though angel armies long to perform the action for which they were created—but without partnership from the earth realm, they will be limited," he continued.

As always, there is a walk of relationship with God in this.

Mitchell told us that Holy Spirit, Jesus, the Father, personal angels as messengers—all of these can help us understand what we are facing. Being able to relate to them about this storm is the first necessary step, but here is what infants do: they run headlong into the storm, shouting and commanding angel armies to stop the storm when perhaps it is not even a storm. Instead, it is a test, or it is a momentary proof of ability—OUR ability. Many of these things arise out of the Father's desire to mature his sons, so pause to find out. Is this for my maturity, and if so, how should I engage it? Or is this a wicked evil set on destruction that needs to be stopped? And realize that:

> *Since I have eyes to see it,*
> *I have authority to stop it.*

What we are doing is this: we are moving against the energy that the storm draws from to remove it and to stop it in its tracks. Because this is spiritual, we must think in spiritual terms. But because it is spiritual, we release the angels into the storm to remove its energy. Angels are equipped to know how to do this. Even when we have a lack of understanding of how it works, they understand how it works. They understand what powers it up. They understand what levels it up. They understand the trade routes that are involved. They understand the illegal legalities that are back doors and wormholes and trades with different realms that are invoking or bringing about this storm.

> *Whether it is a storm*
> *because of witchcraft,*
> *or a storm because of*
> *demonic councils, our ability*
> *to collapse the storm*
> *comes with the help of angels.*

Sometimes a storm is pending, or it is threatening, but it is far off, waiting in the wings to see the response of humans.

---

*Here is what ALWAYS
shuts down storms:
love, unity, hope, worship,
rest, trust, truth, and knowledge.*

When God's people act from these realms, it defeats storms before they begin.

We must try it out. Some people do not understand that to operate as a son or daughter of God, they must engage the spiritual realm from the spirit. They must practice. They must be willing, even in the spirit, to learn, to let the growth curve take place. We cannot be afraid to begin because we are not going to operate as a son perfectly all the time. We grow in this.

Do not be afraid to begin.

That is not a spirit of fear that the Father has given; it is an apprehension that we must be perfect. There was only one who was perfect. His name was Jesus Christ. He had a particular mission on earth, and He fulfilled it with excellence. He dwells by His Spirit in the spirits of those living on planet earth, but the man Jesus was the only perfect man—the only perfect human. This should free us to be able to practice in the spirit with the power given to us in His authority. If we are paying attention to the

Holy Spirit and His prompts, His checks, and His guidance within us, we will not go wrong.

A storm is NOT the will of God. A storm comes to steal, kill, or destroy. It comes to distract. It is costly. It comes to bring with it associated anxieties and displacements.

With that, we began our commissioning for Ezekiel and his team.

> *Holy Spirit, I ask You for assistance to commission the angel Ezekiel, his commanders, and his ranks of armies in the spirit realm. With specificity I address the storm that is trying to erupt around our client. When this person is engaged with our ministry, I commission the angels of God, in the name of Jesus, to quench the storm, calm the humans, collapse all energy frequencies, and bring them to nothing, as well as all backup plans for subsequent storms in the name of Jesus. I loose the angels to their task with God's light, His lightning, and His peace. I bless this person in the name of Jesus. I bless them with what Ephesians 1:18 refers to as 'eyes to see.' I bless them that the eyes of their heart might be enlightened, so that they would know the hope of His calling, and what the riches of the glory of His inheritance in the saints is, and what is the surpassing greatness of His power toward them who believes. I commission Ezekiel and his ranks and commanders to squelch the storm around them. Every time they link with technology to*

> *LifeSpring International Ministries and all its outlets, all emails, classes, coursework, Tuesday night Mentoring Groups, or Wednesday Platinum or Gold meetings, in Jesus' name.*

That was the commissioning relating to one of the two storms. Now it was time to deal with the other storm.

> *I commission Ezekiel, his commanders and ranks in the name of Jesus to squelch and remove all energy from the storm that surrounds our student. I do this based on their commitment as a student to the Facilitator Training Program, to the mentorship class on Tuesday nights, to the connection they make with us as a Platinum Member, and all other connections to LifeSpring International Ministries. I commission the angels to remove all energy from this storm that seeks to distract both the student and LifeSpring International Ministries and all its outlets. I commission Ezekiel to remove all backup plans of this storm. I commission Ezekiel to use God's light, God's lightning, and the peace of God to bring this storm to nothing in Jesus' name.*

Mitchell reminded us, "If you have a storm situation and do not feel overly confident, understand that practice will help you not feel like a toddler.

Not everything is a storm. Occasionally there *are* storms, but not everything is a storm. It takes a great degree of discernment on behalf of the individual to pause and hear and know what to do.

Sometimes a storm happens because we have taken off our armor. In that case, it is not a storm. Rather, we are being buffeted by the enemy because he can see that we took off our armor, so let's put our armor back on!

Finally, do not be afraid of the storm.

We cannot speak to command angels to remove the energy of the storm and collapse a storm realm *if we are afraid of it.*

This also works with the amount of confidence we have. We are not speaking from our own realm; we are speaking out of the realm of the Kingdom. We are speaking from and in the authority of the name of Jesus. We are not thinking, and we are not speaking separated or apart from Him. We are not speaking, hoping that it works. We are speaking, KNOWING that this works. Do we see the difference level in the confidence? Our faith in the knowledge of who He is levels us up in the release of the angelic. They are aware when we speak. They are aware of the degree level of confidence in which we speak. Some of our practice is going to have to be speaking in confidence.

Ezekiel got our attention and pointed out that we needed to deal with another storm. We scanned the horizon in the spirit, moving from side to side and were able to discern another storm that was creating chaos. We commissioned Ezekiel to collapse that storm in the same way as was described earlier.

Ezekiel, we commission you to halt the wind of the storm. We command it to be still, we commission you to bring it to stillness, and destroy all its backup plans in Jesus' name.

Ezekiel pointed out that we had the authority to deal with the storms that *directly affected our realm* as a ministry but did not necessarily have the authority to address other storms affecting the other person(s) even though they may have had some connection to LifeSpring. This does not commission Ezekiel to bring every storm down in that person's realm. It is bringing peace to *this* storm—the one that related to us. He was aware of other storms related to that person that he knows about, but he knows his own boundary and was pointing out to us the difference.

---

*We have authority
over storms affecting us
and our immediate family,
our business, job, or ministry,
but not necessarily over the storms
affecting other people, even if we
have a degree of connection to them.*

With this, our engagement with Mitchell and Ezekiel was ended for this time. We should allow Holy Spirit to speak to us concerning the storms that need to be dealt with personally and follow the steps we have described. We will have nuances to the storms we are facing, but these examples will help us as we go forward in victorious triumph through Jesus Christ.

———·———

Chapter 13

The Good Shepherd

Lydia came with a message for our Platinum members,[11] to share with them at our next meeting. She prompted us to remind them of the goodness of the Good Shepherd. Jesus is a good shepherd. He knows His flock inside and out. He knows their heart cry. He knows their voice. He knows what they need—what they do not need. He is a good shepherd. He tends to the young lamb and the maturing one with equal love and concern. The Good Shepherd carries a rod of protection and guards His flock jealously with the intent to bring them to good pastures.

The Good Shepherd has already brought them to good pastures. He has already provided them with living water, but He *is bringing* them to good pastures, and He *is bringing* them to new waters. He surveys the landscape for where he will bring His flock and He will place them

---

[11] Visit CourtsOfHeavenWebinars.com to find out about our Platinum member program.

so that those among them, whether little lambs or maturing ones, their needs are equally met.

She told us to remember the love of the Good Shepherd for each one in the flock. Remind them they are a flock. They are not *our* flock. They are *the flock of the Lord Jesus Christ*. As the Good Shepherd would, tell them to glory and relax in being known as a member of the flock. This brings a spiritual comfort that can translate to the soul. *He is a good Good Shepherd.*

What do the members of the flock do? They hearken to His Word. They follow His lead. They allow themselves to be led and they perceive the good stream. They perceive the place of abundant pasture.

Here is what Lydia means when we remember how good the shepherd is. Our eye has expectation. Our ear has expectation to receive the good flow of the good stream and the good abundance of the pasture. Many hearts are held back from the expectation of the good stream and the abundant pasture due to losing focus and not being attuned to the voice of the Good Shepherd. He *is* leading His people. He *is* leading his flock. He *has* given His life for the flock. He *has* taken back His life as a shepherd of many flocks. And He *has* abundance streams and pastures.

How does the flock know it is a flock? Because the individual sheep are paying attention to the shepherd. He, the Good Shepherd, makes them a flock. Without a shepherd, they are scattered sheep on a hillside. With a shepherd in the picture, they are a flock. Remember to enjoy the peace and the calmness of the knowledge of understanding that we are His flock because we are each looking to Him.

The needs of the flock are met by the shepherd, not by the flock.

Again, the needs of the flock are not met by the flock. They are met by the shepherd. If we look to another sheep and never hear the voice of the shepherd himself, our membership of the flock is flawed because he cares for each. He speaks to each as a Good Shepherd.

A shepherd reveals the places of abundance. The shepherd reveals the places of refreshing, and he reveals the places of safety. He uses his voice to limit the straying of the individual sheep and is the comforter for the sheep who fall into trouble. His eye is upon his flock always.

A Change of Language

Now, let me change some language. Our spirit—our human spirit—is like the sheep in the shepherd's fold, with the spirits of the flock looking to the shepherd, enjoying the company of others' spirits who are likewise looking to the shepherd.

Little lambs look to other sheep for a while. Mature spirits (mature sheep) look to the shepherd. Newly awakened spirits look for other human spirits and must be taught to look to the Holy Spirit, the other Good

Shepherd. We can take this and exchange the word sheep for spirit and see another layer and level of this way the Good Shepherd leads his flock. He leads us by our spirit, so we must be sure that our spirit is attuned to Him, listening to Him, and following Him.

When all the spirits of those gathered are as one doing that, the release to all the abundance of the goodness of the pastures and the flow of the good stream is released by the Good Shepherd.

Delight in the presence of the Good Shepherd often. We may have to learn what delighting in the Good Shepherd means—delighting ourselves in Him. I am speaking of our spirit. Our spirit delights in His presence. Our spirit is meant to do that. It longs to do that. It is hungry to do that. It is already desiring to drink of the good stream that He leads us to, so learn to delight in the Good Shepherd.

I am the good shepherd; and I know My sheep and am known by My own.[12]

[12] John 10:14

Chapter 14
Observing Traffic Patterns

As I journaled with Heaven recently, I heard the following:

As you continue to share what Heaven shares with you, know that you are breaking ground in the earth and in the lives of my sons and daughters. What you share is vital for their maturing as sons and daughters. They need to learn to live by revelation and truth. Revelation will carry truth, while truth will carry revelation. They are designed by Me to be inseparable. Seeing yourself as I see you is vital to the process of maturing as sons, for only then can you receive true revelation that is unfiltered by your mind—its experiences, its beliefs, its patterns of being and doing.

Revelation that comes from Heaven is unfiltered by falsehood.

In history, many sought revelation, but they sought it while still not being cleansed in their generations or in their own life.

> Purity of revelation cannot come from vessels still filled with debris from their lives and generations.

A cleansing must take place. This arena is a battlefield in the lives of those who read a scripture as present tense when it is, in fact, future tense for that time, because they have not cried out to me to cleanse them of their stuff. They quote that the handwriting of ordinances against us has been done away with,[13] but think that everything is included. The handwriting of the Mosaic law with its 613 rules and regulations—THAT has been done away with. However, some other things are still being worked on.

You must also remember what Paul said when he wrote 'work out your own salvation with fear and trembling.'[14] Apparently, although you will get to Heaven if you are born again and still have stuff to deal with, you are challenged in your full maturing as sons if you hang on to iniquity and secret sins and wicked thought patterns that have never been consciously subjected to the blood of

---

[13] Colossians 2:14
[14] Philippians 2:12

Jesus. David spoke of secret sins[15] and knew they must be dealt with. David experienced much that was before his time and he did so because of his hunger for Me and My presence.

I want you to not be afraid to deal with your stuff. The stuff you see as common to your family line—deal with it. The stuff that plagues you personally—deal with it. Come clean of all of it so that the maturing, the hearing, the seeing, the clarity in revelation—all of this can manifest in your life.

No, you do not have all the answers in your mind, but Heaven does have the answers. Heaven has understandings that are yet to be revealed to you.

Heaven has information that
has yet to be released in the earth.

Just as the information on Collapsing Realms was not due for release until this week, other revelation is waiting in the wings to come forth. Heaven has simply been waiting on maturing ones to open themselves to receive it. That is where you are currently in your life. That is where you are in your walk with Me. Understand that not all things are as they seem to be. Some things have yet to be unveiled—things concerning your

---

[15] Psalm 19:12

experiences, including Adina's[16] experience with what she is dealing with right now. She cannot see the greater weight of glory that awaits on the other side of this ordeal, but it awaits her arrival at that juncture and when the two meet it will be glorious for her and it will bless far more than she can see at this time in her life.

Experiences are not to dictate our life as a rule.

Most experiences are designed to be like an intersection that you pass through. At some intersections you must stop completely, at others you only need to yield or wait for the traffic lights to change, while at others you have freedom to go on through. Do not stop at an intersection where the light is green. Follow the guidelines of traffic rules in those times. Many times, your enemy would have you stop for a green light and go through a red one. He only wants your destruction, either to be hit from behind by continuing traffic or to be broadsided by those passing through the intersection from a different direction.

In your spirit, learn to read the road signs and the traffic lights. Your journey will be much smoother if you do. Do not stop when you should go and do

---

[16] Ron's wife

not go when you should stop or yield. Your spirit knows which is which. Your soul, on the other hand, is still in training. Your soul would want to stop and mope, or complain, or act unruly in other ways. Allow your spirit to direct what you do and how you do it. Live from your spirit. You were designed to do so. The other parts of you—your soul and your body—were designed to facilitate that for you. You and those with you are in re-training mode at this season. As you pass through this season of training and ingraining this pattern into your life, you will find yourself in a much stronger position to receive and walk confidently as a son in My Kingdom. Continue the journey, for it has only just begun.

———·———

Chapter 15
The Outpouring
& Removing the Filters
on the Mind

One Wednesday morning, when we stepped into the realms of Heaven and requested access to the Business Complex, we went to the Help Desk of the complex and asked if there was anything on our schedule.

The attending angel responded, "There is a Sabbath rest on your schedule. A Sabbath rest is warfare." She added, "Sow the seed of a Sabbath rest. Rest from your enemies. Rest from striving against your enemies."

She then handed us a key and instructed us to unlock the door of rest for the ministry. We could then see a calendar and the angel said, "Align with this. Can you align with this? You have already come through the storm. It is over. Now, unlock the door to rest. Unlock rest with the key. Have the mind Christ in this. What was loosed against you has been squelched, and your enemy will hate you taking rest.

[We had just come through a situation where we had to deal with a storm. See the chapter on "Collapsing Storms."]

We then had the sensation as if we were standing under a waterfall. One could feel the weight of the water that hits and how it feels endless when we stand under a waterfall like that. We declared, "I receive this outpouring of rest." It felt like it was filling up the room in which we were sitting.

Lydia approached and said, "It is the outpouring. There is an outpouring in the earth right now.

Whoever will put out their buckets can partake of it.

"It is being poured out from Heaven. It is timed by Heaven. Notice the calendar. It is *this* outpouring."

Lydia said, "You are feeling this like the outpouring of a waterfall, a steady stream of a lot of water released all at one time so that when you stand under it, you can barely stand up and it hits you on your shoulders and on the head. It is relentless because of the force with which it is falling."

The other thing it felt like was that the measure of the rate of the flow of the outpouring was great—maybe not like Niagara Falls, but consistent. It was not a trickle. We did not know how to measure that flow rate, but it was consistent, and it was going to move things. There was something about this outpouring—it was a spiritual outpouring. We could feel it coming from Heaven. It was in the spirit, and **it was going to move objects that we had thought were immobile.** We had considered them stationary. We had considered that we had to go around them. Yet, the rate of flow of this outpouring is going to move those objects. Lydia did not say it was going to move them out of the way; she told us it was *moving* them, so what we thought was stationary is now moveable.

Lydia told us that when the saints of the earth join with Holy Spirit to release the movement of those things once thought stationary and speak to them, we will be moved by the power of God. We will be moved by His movement. We cannot stay stationary. We will move. We will change. We will change where we are. We will change our location. We will be moved. We will be moved out. We will be moved aside. We will be moved.

There is a great release of the power of the saints of God from the verbal agreement with what God is doing right now for the release of those things that will now be moved. Say to the earth, "You will now be moved. Stationary objects who have planted themselves against the movement of God, you will now be moved. You will move aside."

Also, in this waterfall is a great amount of faith. We are accustomed to seeing and experiencing faith that has an expected outcome and goal like this. We can apply our faith to it.

This faith feels different though. It feels like a faith flow of Heaven's movement for objects to move that have considered themselves planted. The faith is just *that* they move. Usually, we think of that type of faith as a thing that we can name or a something that can be. This does not have a name to it. It is just movement. It is faith *for movement.*

It releases the faith for movement. On the heels of this move of God, we will need to watch because, from the earth realm, it will manifest in what we call a timeline, but also on the heels of that movement will come change. That change must be accommodated.

Become accustomed to change.

Declare ourselves possessing the mind of Christ. Declare ourselves *in* the mind of Christ *with* the mind of Christ in us.

---

*Declare that the change
is easily navigated.*

As we declare that the mind of Christ is in us, and that we are *in* the mind of Christ, that we *have* the mind of Christ—reach up and grab the mind of Christ. This is the *dunamis*[17] resurrection power of the understanding of His height of dominion. It His Royal kingship. It is His resurrection power.

We could also see lightning in the waterfall and were told that those are lightnings of God. As the flow comes out, as the outpouring comes out of Heaven in the fall of that water—as it is falling, there are what looks like lightning bolts. It looks like lightning bolts in the water, mixing with it, and somehow it relates to energy light. We have the energy of the water. We have the energy of the light frequency. We asked Lydia, "What do we do about that?"

Lydia responded, "This is the increase of His power on the earth. It is mixed in the outpouring. It has to do with the opening of men's understanding. This is the goodness of God to His children, the goodness of the Creator who creates and cannot be stopped. Do we feel the goodness of the Father who creates and can never be stopped? He *never* can be stopped. The enemy *thought* he could stop God. It is the ultimate joy of all things working out according to His plan. He has *never* been thwarted, and He enjoys His victory."

---

[17] Definition of the Greek word "*dunamis*": #1411—miraculous power, might, strength. Usage: physical power, force, ability, efficacy, energy, powerful deeds, deeds showing physical power, marvelous works (Strong)

We said, "Even the heinous awful activity of evil is minuscule in the face of the power of His victory and when the saints catch wind of this—"

Lydia interjected, "Combine that with His love. Then thrones are shaken—whatever evil thrones Satan pretends to think he has, they are completely shaken. There is going to come a time where men's minds are not focused on the ruination of the enemy as he tries to bring all things evil to the forefront of the mind, because they are going to be so overtaken with the power and love and goodness of the Father.

"I will tell a secret: this heals. This knowledge heals. It aligns. It straightens what is crooked. It brings into alignment what is missing. It retrieves things that are missing. It attracts like a magnet to it things that are missing and adds to itself so that it becomes whole. This has to do with the fragmentation of light. The enemy has illegally used the fragmentation of light and he is about to be stopped. The understanding of the wholeness of the light of God in the hearts and spirits of man—even the belief systems and the cellular brain structure of light is going to be rearranged."

Think of the cells in our body like pools and receive the light there.

We saw waves and waves and waves, like tsunami waves crashing over a vision of people standing in the Father's love. It is the grasp of His love. It is the ability to grasp His love. It is the ability to grasp the power of love from a beneficial Father who benefits us with all that He is, always a hundred percent consistently with it, never stopping.

Now this is different because, whereas the waterfall moves things, these waves are large waves, like the kind that come and curl over and then they crash and then another one forms, but these waves are soft. They are large, but they are soft. They are a force that brings something in, but they are not the kind that just crashes.

Lydia explained that these are the billowing waves of His love. It is very exciting. It is an exciting time to be alive now and to stand and enjoy the benefits of the Father, who is our creator and to appropriate His faith, His love, His majesty, and to see ourselves in this frame. We represent Him. An unlocking is coming.

Filters on the Mind

One of the things that will be moved aside by this outpouring of the waterfall are the filters on the mind. There are filters on the mind. I am not talking about the brain; I am talking about the mind. There have been filters on the mind. It has been an ancient work of an enemy of God.

The filters are going to move. We are going to find that the filters on the mind, these filters on the thoughts, are far more moveable and malleable than what we have experienced. The clouds of witnesses have known about this coming, and they are watching. It excites them to investigate it.

It is a promise of God and we are to share it like we would share a promise. Its purpose is to instill hope—because of His goodness, because He hears the cry of His children, because He knows their hearts—but also let it instill holiness and the beauty of His Throne's dominion: that He is God and there is no other, and that His ways are not human ways. Let holiness settle in us, around us, and on us. This holiness is the pleasure of being known. Remember, scripture says, "He knows all things."

---

*Learn to luxuriate
in the luxury of being known.*

This is connected to the verse in scripture in the Old Testament where it says, "When you get up, when you lie down, when you come and when you go, when you do this, and when you do that." Luxuriate in the luxury that we are known. Let that become personal. Let the knowledge of us being known become personal. Let it come closer to us. Let it come deeper to us. Let it come broader in us. Let this come *in* us. We are known. We *are* known.

The word "known" feels like not just known, but when we are known, it is like when we have a favorite sweater and we put it on. We love having it on. We love how it feels and we know what it makes us feel like. We know how close it is. We feel as if we know what every fiber feels like. That is why it is a favorite. It is like God wears us. He knows us so well. He wears us like we wear that favorite sweater or that favorite sweatshirt or that favorite piece of clothing. Just think of that. Why do we turn to that? Because we feel comfortable, we feel satisfied. We feel well. We feel at leisure. We feel at pleasure. We feel all of that wearing a favorite garment and God wears us like that. That is how we are known. We *are* known. He has pleasure in that. He has put Himself in us and put us on.

Imagine the Body of Christ having this mind of Christ concerning the enjoyment of the Godhead, as the Father puts on those that He has redeemed unto Himself. He has put us on. He knows us like this. We can know our known-ness. We can know ourselves like He knows us. The only way to know ourselves is to know us as He knows us.

The only way to do that is to commune and have His mind. Some of the trouble has been the filters from the fruit of the wrong tree, from the filters of the world, from the filters of doctrines of demons and from the filters of fear, loneliness, inadequacy, and the fear of not being supported. He has already rescued us from these things.

Let our understanding blossom in the fact that He has already rescued us from these things.

As we see ourselves already rescued from these things, our mind can change our outlook. As our mind aligns with the mind of truth, a different outcome plays out because we have linked to truth—truth is the outcome.

Remember how we were told "nothing is hard because nothing is impossible"? This is the associated knowledge with that.

The anticipation of goodness decreases fear.

Our mind chooses the anticipation of goodness. Our mind can choose the anticipation of a good outcome and receive the outplay of the goodness and the kindness and the power of God. Focus only on these things—our spirit will help us focus on this.

If *this* is our constant stance and our come from is the anticipation of goodness—it does not mean that we cannot have any knowledge that the enemy is at work over here trying this, or trying to pull this stunt here, or is holding someone in captivity. Do not take this to mean that if we focus on the good, we do not have the knowledge of how to defeat the enemy, because we can see what he is doing but we are not focused on that. We are not. Our ears are closed to the frequencies of the enemies attack, but not from the frequency of how God is going to overcome it or how He is about to release the solution or strategy for it or even cancel it.

For some of us, the filter that just popped up in our mind was how people do not see or they do not think they see the movement. That is a filter—so if we focus on the good expectation of the outcome and we move the filter aside and we say, "The movement of God is everywhere," that is changing one's mind. We can feel that in our brain. We see God's movement everywhere. God is a moving God; He is always moving.

> *Father, whatever that filter in my mind, or my belief system is, or wherever my heart comes from, I come out of agreement with it. I come out of alignment with it. I ask the Father to judge through the blood of Jesus between me and it. And I put it [the mind filter] under the blood of Jesus Christ and under my feet. And I say to that filter, "You will never appear on me again." I release myself from this mind filter in Jesus' name.*

Every time we see a filter, we speak to that filter. A lot of humanity operates out of these filters that are on the mind and this is what God is releasing the power to move.

Scriptures About the Mind:

1 Corinthians 2:16

2 Corinthians 3:14

2 Corinthians 4:4

Philippians 4:7

134

Chapter 16
Embracing Change

Change is where we are. Do not think it is just "change is here." Change IS here! Do we not know it? We are in a new cycle and *new* means change because our sense of movement is like going to a place we have not known.

---

*This is both **the era**
and **the season** for change.
Begin to become comfortable
with change.*

Our soul realm takes comfort from things being the same, but the spirit of the man—the spirit of a human, is receptive to change; it needs change—it brightens with the nuance of change. Speak to the soul and tell the soul to enjoy change. Tell the soul, "You will now enjoy change. It is time to embrace change. It is time to call change good."

Humans are troubled by things that are new, but...

---

*The spirit of a redeemed son of God
is engaged and intrigued
by change and the new.*

The change that is upon us is planned. This is a planned change. There is a change of maneuverings and change works on behalf of the saints because it keeps the enemy guessing. Change is healthy. Change keeps our frequency brighter and more fluid.

Rigidity from the soul realm entraps the spirit of a man. Rigidity is comfortable to the soul. Rigidity is not exciting. Rigidity, routine, and being halted or stopped—these are symbols of death and dying.

---

*Enjoy the movement forward
to new things.*

Embrace new, for all life is in change and newness.

---

*Change and newness
are the definition of life.*

Our soul sees these things as negative, but we have the capacity to flip them to view them from the positive, to view them from the embrace. Learn to love them. As we learn to love what is changing, the maneuver of changing is a weapon against the enemy. Become agile, adaptable, flexible. These are spiritual terms that our spirit understands and our soul labors with. However, as we have learned, the spirit realm is the higher dimension from which we came. Therefore, our spirit understands this, but our spirit needs the assistance of Holy Spirit and spirit beings like Ezekiel, and like the cloud of witnesses, and like the varied assortment of angelic beings to feel watered and move forward. The soul will try and make us feel like we have moved forward when we have not moved forward because it will give us a false signal that we have changed, but we did not change.

Change happens in the spirit realm first.

The spirit realm is a wave link of frequencies of movement and light and vibrations. The spirit realm experiences the consistent release of cycles and movement that excite our spirit—it makes our spirit vibrate. Not like they get excited emotionally, but that our spirits generate energy: sound, light, vibrations, undulating movements, and cycles of change that are both large and compartmentalized. All are necessary for life. Be flexible. Be adaptable. Be what the Father made us to be. We are adaptable. We are changeable. We are momentum. We are a frequency. We are a vibration. We are a movement. We are a growth. We are a new thing. It is the principle of the creation expanding itself ever and evermore because at one time it was spoken.

We are going to have to learn to live this way. We are going to have to learn to live this way so that our body does not attract and hold on to anxiety, stress, and worry. Even the CourtsNet students need to understand their capacity to embrace the change that has come near them.

The rigidity of the soul realm is to be comfortable in what it knows, and we see the spirit of a man become vibrational to the point of being fluid—like water when we give permission to our spirit to flow that way, or when we tell the soul, "You are not in charge of this." Rather, "I will live by spirit movement, vibration, fluidity, flexibility, and adaptability because I can." We can because this is who we are.

The spirit realm is a higher dimension than where we came from and in which we were reawakened and born again from, and from which our soul can now view—as through a lens—the audacity of living from one's spirit.

> *It is audacious to live from one's spirit while yet on the earth. This makes us Kingdom citizens of two realms.*

Which realm is greater? The spirit realm is greater in *every* respect. Living from two realms is an invitation to us. It is an open door. The work of Christ and what occurs is the manifestation of the Kingdom of God into the physical realm because we have chosen to live in the spirit realm from our spirit man.

Chapter 17

A Word About Surrender

Ezekiel met us and explained, "I have come from the realms and much observation of time and not time. I have ranks that are taking back territory. It is time to take back territory from the enemy that has been stolen from the Body of Christ." We saw Ezekiel moving quickly as if flying with his sword outstretched. "Is there a purpose in my needing to see this?" we asked.

He replied, "To know the Father's might. To know the effect of angels on your behalf and to keep in the forefront of your understanding how much light and the Kingdom of Light overwhelms darkness because it has not gotten a chance. It does not have a chance when the sons and daughters of God are releasing angels, collaborating with them in tandem and advancing the Kingdom of God.

"You look with natural eyes to the natural world and see the projection of the enemy. When you look with spirit realm eyes to the realm of the spirit and engage

Heaven, or like now, as you engage me, I can portray to you the truth of the scenario."

At that moment, we could suddenly see the globe and saw China and watched arrows raining down.

"Whose arrows are these?" we asked.

He replied, "These are the arrows of the Army of Light." He said, "Look more closely at them. They are exceptionally fine, and they are made of gold. The battle against this principality (over China) is engaged currently."

We could not see the angels that were releasing the arrows but could see the arrows which were falling like rain. It did not appear that there was even a space that did not have an arrow in it.

Ezekiel explained that he can show us the news of Heaven. He can show us the display of God's might, power, and glory as He will have the earth. He *has* the earth, and He will *have* the earth and *all* its occupants.

He stopped explaining any more about that subject and said he wanted to talk about the word "surrender.

To an angel, this is a great mystery, for the sons and daughters of God have truly surrendered their lives to the King of Kings. Angels were not wired with the ability to surrender. Angels do not have this choice. We need to understand that angels truly find this mysterious. The way we surrender our realms, our lives and our will to the Father is a most remarkable thing. We do not often hear of angels crying, but we often cry at the beauty of a surrendered heart to Jesus. We may wonder "Why is this?" It is because it is the pathway of entrance to the Glory realm and to the place of reflecting the Father's Glory from the 3-D realm.

Angels know that the 3-D realm—the natural earth—needs the portal connection to the spiritual realm that a surrendered heart and life affords. We shine more with His Glory than we know. When we surrender our lives in exchange for His, and as the Holy Spirit takes His place within our being, and we are in the process of being changed, the light that we emit as a surrendered one to the King terrifies darkness and causes it to flee. Why else do we suppose the enemy wants to blind us and to cause our light to be under a veil, or like scripture says, 'under a basket'? When we walk not knowing who we are, or when we walk in self-righteousness without a surrendered heart to this King of Glory, we do not fulfill our purpose on planet earth. But as we walk with a surrendered realm, a surrendered life, and a surrendered heart to the King, allowing His Spirit to flow from us, we emanate light simply by being surrendered, and to the physical realm, everywhere we go, we light it up.

This has been portrayed in movies, documentaries, and fiction where the silhouette of a person on screen is just white light. There are films that depict a super-sight where we can see through things using goggles and we see a human in a container, and we can see them as a white silhouette. This is Heaven's view. Those who are surrendered to the Lord are like this. The light can be seen by spiritual beings.

> *His light in us is a thing, and it can be seen by spiritual beings.*

It is the light of His shining. It is the light of His arising. It is the light of His Glory. It is also the brightness that shines from within us that even the physical realm responds to.

The 3-D realm responds to this supernatural light within us, and the children of God are learning to release this light and the glory of His power and might with more frequency.

As we do courtroom work for the removal of the legal rights of Satan to bloodline iniquities, based on those verdicts of righteousness, the frequency of the glory of His light within us shines brighter, and angels see this. This is what was in operation as the throngs of people were drawn to Jesus when He was on planet earth. They were drawn irresistibly to His light. Why? Because they had the capacity to have the same light and Jesus' healing and miracles released their capacity to shine brightly through their belief, through their agreement with who He was and with the assurance of hope.

Garzan's Message

Garzan appeared a few moments later and had a message for us. We received the message and invited him to read it to us.

Hark! Hearken to a great light of the glory of Jesus Christ. Let it be known on earth that His kingdom will come and cannot be stopped. Let it be known that a turning has begun.

To the children of God comes the message of opening their mouth to begin to repeat the word of the will of Yahweh. A turning and a turning has come and will not be deflected nor overcome. A turning and a turning has begun. As a new leaf budding from a tree and turning to the sunlight, so is the turning and turning of this decree. Time will align, both time on earth and time in Heaven, for the joyous occasion of the turning. Celebrate as His people and rejoice with faithful hope that the turning of things has occurred and so shall it be.

Ezekiel then began to give some interpretation to what Garzan had spoken and explained to us to let the surrendered part of our heart receive the joy of this announcement. It is an announcement from Kingdom realms regarding time. See this as done in our physical 3-D timeline realm and allow our spirit to rejoice as Abraham rejoiced in the promised son.

Many traumas exist in the people of God which hope deferred has caused. These have become walls against the faithfulness of God. Yield and surrender the walls that have been erected against the truth and might of God, so that we can rejoice with hopeful expectation in His decree and in what He will do, for He is not a man that He should lie.[18] Let Holy Spirit comfort the places of trauma that hope deferred has left but rise up and command every intruder of hope deferred to leave our realms, so that we may celebrate and rejoice in anticipation of the manifestation of His Words. Again, God does not lie!

The discussion morphed into the subject of time and thinking dimensionally. We were encouraged to think dimensionally, not in 3-D. Time can change...and change again.

All we must do is believe.

Remember, we must hear the voice of God. We must be in dialogue with the Godhead. We must hear Him speak strategies and plans to us—whether in the night season or in the day. Doing so is crucial in this hour. Hear the Lord. Record what He says. Count on his promises. Let our faith and our joy rise into celebration.

Hope deferred often comes because we have not heard the Word of God for ourselves. Personally, we

---
[18] Numbers 23:19

have not taken the time to get in His presence and hear His word for us personally. Therefore, we have drawn inappropriate conclusions about what the words that others have heard mean. This drawing of wrong conclusions is the place where hope deferred squats.

We have mind conclusions. We have soul conclusions. We have emotional conclusions. What we need to operate from is the spiritual oneness conclusion. That is a process of a journey with each footfall taken in faith and belief. Believe the goodness of God. Believe the goodness of God in the land of the living.

———·———

Chapter 18

Abraham on Surrender

On one of our engagements with Heaven, the council we met with had a special guest—the father of faith, Abraham. We asked for his input as we met together. The honor that was bestowed on him by those gathered was noticeable. Abraham had this to share with us. He began,

> *A uniqueness of body, soul, and spirit capacity is being released. The sons of men and the sons of God will have a showdown. Those filled with the light frequency of His Glory can engage their citizenship of Heaven for maximum benefit. The world's glory will not remain; it is passing now even quickly. How you engage this transition results in your ability to see yourself for who you really are—the sons of men versus the sons of God. There is a showdown that must take place. It takes place internally in each individual, and it will take place in bodies of people (groupings of people).*

There is a new awakening forming itself inside the sons of God, such that has not been on earth yet. This comes through the realm of God's sons. It comes to the realms of God's sons from the inside to the outside. The sons of God become aware of how they are changing internally. They become aware of the fact that they are being changed internally. Their systems are coming online in a manner of speaking with the systems of Heaven. Their heart is like a gate, choosing for them in a way that they will go. Surrendered hearts are like surrendered lives and trust becomes the issue, whether trust in oneself as sons of men, or trust in God as sons of God.

A precipice looms ahead where another choosing happens. There are many angel armies who have been waiting in the wings to assist the sons of God to surrender and let God be who He is among them. This will be a time like when Moses went to meet God on the mountain, considering himself already dead. He fully surrendered everything that he was in the natural to encounter God in everything He was being displayed as, fully trusting that God would be responsible for the outcome. Jesus, in like manner, surrendered everything, trusting the Father to oversee the outcome. Your day will be filled with like opportunity—trusting God for the outcome.

> *A lot can take place when you trust God for the outcome.*

I trusted Him with the outcome of Isaac. Sons of God are about to understand the faithfulness of God—not for how He responded to their desire, but for how He responds to His own plan—to the faithfulness of his own plan, to the faithfulness of His own being. God is faithful to Himself.

> *Lead your life in contentment with the Spirit of God.*

Learning to live your life with the contentment of the Spirit of God will feel like your life takes on new definition. It will feel like life is being redefined. Surrender to the fact that there are many things you have not been told. Surrender to the fact that there are many things that will not be told. Surrender to the fact that there are many things that will not initially run according to your own judgments. Surrender and follow.

Chapter 19
Angelic Engagement

Ezekiel began a sidenote by saying, "There are some reading your books and they read about me, and they are trying to engage me. It would be good for you to talk with them about their need to engage their own angels, the angel(s) assigned to them as their personal angel, but other angels assigned to them as well. There are other angels assigned to them too—not all angels are going to have a relationship with them in that they talk to them. But use the phrase 'the angels assigned to me.'"

Ezekiel pointed out that when we speak of or to Ezekiel, it is because he is the angel of *this* ministry. Some, as they read the books, are trying to engage with Ezekiel at the level we are engaging with him. This is inappropriate.

Ezekiel reminded us, "Just remember, there is an order of angels. All things in the angelic world are ordered. I am being very plain. It is not appreciated when things are out of order or tried to be entered." We are to follow the leading of the Spirit of God within us. We are to receive teaching from the Spirit of God and direction, leading, and prompting. Ask Holy Spirit to reveal to us our angels. Many are operating immaturely in this, where they are trying *from their soul* realm to make a connection to an angel. This is not how it works.

> *Our human spirit and Holy Spirit oneness connect with the realm of angelic activity.*

We should not be impatient to meet our angel, *nor should we agree with the enemy* that our angel is not present. Many angels are present, and backup angels are always present. Do not fall to the lie of the enemy that he has captured more angels than have been captured. This is false. Be discerning in your spirit with Holy Spirit, the author of discernment.

If you believe an angel to be captured when it is *not* captured, this hurts that angel and causes a warfare in that angel's realm. We must believe what Holy Spirit is showing us about our angel.

> *Do not make assumptions from our soul and intellect but be surrendered to Holy Spirit's truth.*

A plot is afoot against the sons and daughters of God who are learning about angels to make them think their angel is not present or is captured. This is a ploy to bring warfare in the angelic realm. Resist this. There are many contributions to why we have things taking place in our realm that have nothing to do with our angel. Be discerning, seek Holy Spirit and the Kingdom of God. Ask for help at the Help Desk. Do not fall to the lie of the enemy from our soul realm, telling us that our angel is missing. Every angel who is missing is noted in Heaven and the battle is working itself out for the rescue of these angels. Occasionally we will see an angel missing, but this is not the norm. The enemy is plotting to make us think that it is normal, so that he has a greater inroad into the battle—into the skirmish.

Our belief, as we grow in these things and mature in these things, is very necessary. We must believe in our angel. Having faith that angels have been assigned to us increases the ability of our angels. We are linked that way somehow. Remember, there *are* enough angels.

———·———

Chapter 20
Shifting Paradigms

We had gathered with a council in the realms of Heaven to discuss some things related to the ministry. Included in the council were Lydia, Mitchell, Malcolm, George, Alicia, and an unidentified special guest.

There are shifting paradigms in the earth right now. People are beginning to see the level of their involvement that will be needed to live as Kingdom sons. Men and women in white linen were always meant to be involved in the action of the physical earth and of the realization of the need for participation in natural things. People are beginning to awaken to this part of their sonship. People are still awakening from quite a lot of religious tradition. They are shaking off from their slumber, but just like when we wake up in the natural and we begin to consider what is ahead of us for our day, people are saying "I know I need to do something different, but I do not know what the 'different' is yet."

There are a lot of layers and levels of this related to timing in the earth and related to breakthroughs there that are still coming. There is also a whole lot of grace right now for people to awaken to new thinking and new thoughts about who they are in Christ, about what God wants from his sons and daughters, what the leading of the Spirit is directing them into, and this is a good question: "What is the Spirit of God leading me into?"

Define this from the difference of the world. "What is the world leading me into? What is the emotion? What are my emotions wanting to lead me into? What is the Spirit leading me into? When the Spirit leads me into a thing, how does that filter out in spiritual terms, physical realm terms, and emotional terms?"

What is the leading?

One of the best questions that people can ask themselves right now is: "What is the leading? What is Holy Spirit leading me into? What is Holy Spirit leading me into today? What is Holy Spirit leading me into this week? What is Holy Spirit leading me to do or say by word or deed, and where is He *not* leading me? Where do I sense He is *not* leading me to do that?"

Distractions

Our distractions can come from our soul. Our distraction can come from the world. I am talking about all the available information around us. If Holy Spirit is not leading us into the available information, then we are being distracted. There is a time for it, but it can be a distraction. On all the devices that humans use, all the sources of information, all sorts of outlets of information that people are using to distract themselves with, it would be beneficial to realize that this is a distraction from the Spirit of God that dwells in His people.

I will say it very plainly; the enemy needs our attention to distract. He wants to *own* our attention.

Pay attention to what is owning our attention.

The demands of the physical can own our attention. The demands of the world and its voice can demand our attention. Where is our attention? At what level are we giving attention to Holy Spirit? When we give attention to Holy Spirit, all the rest will go well with us.

Where we get distracted, we are being conformed to the world.

This will be some of the defining of things between the sons and daughters of God in Jesus, and those who are being conformed to the world, being depressed by the world, being told what to think, and being herded into conformity and distraction.

> *What we give attention to*
> *will make a difference in these days.*

There are even some things in us in our natural realm that are demanding attention, but these things do not *need* that much attention. They need only a little bit of attention. Instead, we are giving it a great deal of attention. In this, I am not talking about the voice of the media. I am really talking about the demands of physical life. Give these things only a little bit of attention, so that we are available to give our attention something else – something more prominent. What are we giving our attention to?

> *We are giving our life essence*
> *away to something*
> *when we give it attention.*

There is plenty of life essence from the Father who upholds our breath. Then there are those who want to steal it from us which feels like it is stealing our energy. I am not talking about the energy we get from food. I am talking about the energy of the light of our spirit man that comes from Heaven. It will prove out well for those who sit down and analyze what they are giving attention to. "To what *am I* giving my attention?" Allow Holy Spirit to direct our attention.

> *Holy Spirit will counsel us regarding*
> *the direction of our attention*
> *when we are willing to surrender*
> *our attention to Him.*

Our life is not our own. We have been hidden in Christ Jesus. Finding the path of abundance in hidden realms and the seeing realm comes through the spirit of the man—the awakened spirit of a son or daughter of God who allows their focus and their attention to be drawn to what the Holy Spirit is leading them to and showing to them.

> *In our world, this will take*
> *some time and surrender*
> *to come to the conclusion*
> *of what Holy Spirit is leading to.*

This is a big shift—a big shift within one's being—within a mind, within a heart, to do that.

There are more things changing than we are aware of. Some of the things that are changing are on the inside of people. Things on the inside of people are changing—what they look for, what they want. There is just a lot changing on the inside of humanity.

> *Do not be afraid of seismic change.*

Have no fear about change.

Change only brings about something that has not been seen before or partaken of. It is good for our spirit, soul, and body that change take place. Change is not negative. Change is neutral. It is how we stand in the change—how we experience what is changing that matters. It is our choice how to embrace it that makes the difference to us, to the quality of our lives.

Chapter 21
Encouragement to Believe

I want to encourage us to believe. A message as simple as this will get swept to the wayside if we are not careful, but I want to encourage us *to believe*. Many are not believing (because of their distraction level) that learning to feed oneself from the spirit is necessary.

Going back to no belief is hard.

---
*We have in Jesus the ability
to change our mind
and to think in a new way about
any topic that we have been
chewing on in the soul.*

That topic must be presented to our spirit man, because our spirit man has a choice that will override the soul. Our spirit must be given the choice to decide what it will think about a thing, and our spirit can change the direction of the flow of our thoughts for things not to be hard and not to be impossible. We must engage our right of choice to believe and choose how we want to think about a thing. We must choose how we want to think about it. Then we must face the fact that we are thinking in a perspective, in a path, in a direction, and we must stop and say, "Is this the direction I want my thoughts to be in?" Because if we do not choose for our thoughts to be there, we can change the direction of our thoughts. This is the function of our spirit man of overriding the soul realm so that we are making the willful intent of choice from our spirit to think a different thought about a thing, a person, a circumstance, or an event. Some say this is the ascended path of choice, but it begins when we stop and think, "Do I want these thoughts I am thinking, or do I want a different set of thoughts?" We can choose the thoughts we will have.

Our spirit in oneness relationship with the Father, the Son, and the Holy Spirit gives us this right of choice and from this comes the change in the frequency of the physical realm vessel, which is our body. Making choices from our spirit is often resisted. Do we know who it is resisted by? It is resisted by Christians. It is from all the wrong associations and wrong teachings that we got when we were young, but we can learn a new way rather than woundedness or fear. These two things will prevent those focusing on woundedness or focusing on fear from changing their thoughts. Woundedness or fear will keep us from considering, "Do I want the thought I'm thinking?"

The world is full of things telling us how we should think. Everywhere we see things telling us how we should think. The sons and daughters of God need to consider, "Is this what the Holy Spirit is telling me to think about this?"

It is as if there are loudspeakers on planet earth directing our thoughts, but the sons and daughters of God, in oneness with Jesus Christ, through the infilling power of the Holy Spirit, have the right to make a new thought to think or to consider, "Am I thinking the thought I choose to think?" or "Am I thinking a thought that I've fallen into thinking or I've been taught to think?" or "Am I thinking the thought that has been presented to me to think? I choose with the willful intent of my spirit man to overcome this and think the thought that I want to think."

This is taking ground back from the enemy, but it is an awakening to our truest identity in Christ and to our seamless oneness with Him. It is a good time to say hallelujah. Hallelujah!

Chapter 22
Rise Up!

On this beautiful morning, we had accessed the Help Desk of the Business Complex of Heaven to discover if anything was in the ministry's Outstanding Folder that we needed to take care of. The angel at the desk, whom we had seen often, began to share with us. She explained that she was the angel we would most often see at the Help Desk because she had an assignment to our ministry.

At this point, we could envision shifting, blowing sand. As Heaven often does, they illustrate what they are going to speak to us about. An angel said, "All things are moving together according to the plan of God. Many things are shifting—moving."

Then we saw the strings of a large upright harp, like a floor model that is five to six feet tall, and we could see the end of the harp where the thicker (bass tones) were vibrating. The vibration of the larger strings are larger movement frequencies which are moving, moving,

moving. It is a good thing. It is vibrating according to Heaven's movement. The deeper strings or the lower tones are the stronger shifts of atmosphere. When these play from Heaven, the result in the physical world is what we call a shaking. We call it movement with many levels of movement involved—national level movements, movements on family levels, movements on individual levels, movements in hearts, movements in manner of thought, even the shifting of many layers and the shifting of hearts. The effect of this heavenly bass tone in spiritual dimensions cause heartstrings of humanity, which are tied to emotion and tied to movement because things are often moved by the desire of one's heart as Heaven plays the deeper bass tones to synchronize. As the bass tones are played, the heart movement of God's people are synchronized.

The movement of the heartstrings of Heaven, the deep tones of Heaven, causes the mind of Christ to begin to resonate in the heart of God's people, and they are afforded greater wells of thinking as the Father thinks, emoting as He emotes, which then equates to focusing on what He is focusing on, gazing on what He is gazing on. This is timely, due to many clocks and the many times of Heaven.

An angel appeared and began to declare boldly:

Command, command, command! Command the day! Command your heart! Command the things of God to appear in the earth realm. Command them at the hands of angel armies. Command them by verbal release. Command because Jesus is the Captain of the Host. As He lives and dwells in you, command the alignment of seasons and times on earth as it is in Heaven.

Conquer! Conquer! Conquer! All His foes will be conquered by the verbal release of God's people. Announce the Conquering King. Announce the coming move. Conquer enemy tactics. Conquer the presumption of the enemy. Conquer the presumption of defeated foes and defeated kingdoms. Conquer them by faith's release. Verbally command and conquer the enemies of God. Put them under your feet.

Much will be poured out in coming days, but it is wise for the people of God to request a refreshing when they are aware of their need. Personal requests to be filled up with the living water of God is so important for God's people. Our body (our flesh) and our soul require the constant refreshing and filling of the Holy Spirit in our spirit being. If we are a vessel filled with the living water of the Holy Spirit, filled with the Spirit of God, filled with the knowledge of His presence, filled with the sensation of His movement, then we resonate what He resonates.

Deep tones are coming from Heaven and are filling our spirits. Our spirit now has an ease. It finds itself more harmonious because we resonate what Heaven resonates, then the soul does not have to strive because the soul is paying attention to the spirit and the body undergoes a synchronization.

Every time we gather, many vessels are filled in joint harmony, focused on being filled and staying filled with the Spirit of God. We move with greater ease, with greater velocity, and with greater impact and greater miracles. Therefore, the soul can find rest here.

What the enemy does is vex the soul and the soul feels that vexation.

If the soul is trained to rely on the spirit, which is our design, then our spirit is being filled with the Spirit of God and His living water by simply asking for the living water, and by the spirit focusing its spirit sight on the presence of God—this is where the spirit feels that nothing is impossible. The soul begins to understand that nothing is hard. More spiritual activity—spirit forward, spirit first—this is a central theme of what is available to God's people. When we sense the waning of our spirit being forward, that signals the need for getting refilled.

Speaking in tongues is essential.

Taking time to be quiet with the Lord is essential, as is taking time to follow the unction of the Holy Spirit in our daily activities and breaking free of soul routines that have no advantage to us.

> *Soul routines often get in the way of the spirit operating by the unction of the Holy Spirit and they will ultimately clash.*

> *The soul must learn to surrender to the spirit's function in order to continue spirit-forward living.*

Many people are learning many things about this right now. There is healing for the soul, and this comes much quicker when the spirit has been filled—when the spirit man is full, when the discussion of what the spirit is saying among us is highlighted, primary, forward, and given permission. Joy then returns from the spirit and is translated to the soul. Our soul may be surprised that it can have joy amid transition, change, movement, shifting sands, blowing sand, and the deep that calls to deep—the deep tones of Heaven calling to the deep tones in our spirit man.[19] The deep tone of Heaven grounds us.

> *The deep calling to deep gives us the firm foundation that we are standing on in spiritual realms.*

---

[19] Psalm 42:7

Rock solid is another way to say it.

Lydia had been talking to us about shakings when Ezekiel joined us and explained that there is a lot still shaking in the earth. We may have thought shaking was over after the recent difficulty with the exposure of viral weapons, but it is all part of the same shaking. Do we know what happens when we shake people? They wake up.

There is a great awakening happening.

Ezekiel had a warrior-like in appearance and the footwear he was wearing were not boots because they were more conformed to his foot, but they had spikes that were about four or five inches long which taper. They were wide at the base where they attached to his footwear and tapered to very needle-like points. They were also in the heel area. The spikes stick out of the back and on the side and on the bottom as well. They were like the footwear a Roman gladiator might wear.

Ezekiel explained that the visual was given so we could comprehend what he was doing. He wears this footwear when about warring functions. It signals that he is ready for action. He is on alert—not on standby. He is on call and "all-hands-on-deck."

We noticed that his wings also looked different. They looked like a deep blue metal. On the bottom of the wing, where it tapers off, they had a titanium look to them.

Ezekiel elaborated, "This is a form of weapon as well. I show you what you need to know and what you are permitted to know. We are ranks of an army, and we not only take our cue from your activity, but we take our cue from the commander of angel armies, King Jesus, the Lord of All. There are developments going on that we are aware of before you are, and we must prepare for these and take our mission from the King."

He described to us what occurred on the Day of Pentecost recorded in Acts 2 (after Jesus had ascended) when the Holy Spirit was poured out in the upper room.

"It was a momentous day of much battle, but not because we were trying to win. We had won since time immemorial, but your foe never admits defeat, so we consistently must remind him of his defeat. You would do well to remind him too."

Get our game on and remind the enemy of his defeat.

Praising God reminds the enemy of his defeat. Celebrating our victory reminds the enemy of his defeat. Praying in faith with full belief reminds the enemy of his defeat. Activating spiritual realm dynamics reminds the enemy of his defeat. Engaging angel armies reminds the enemy of his defeat. Engaging Counsel Rooms of Heaven reminds the enemy of his defeat. He will battle until the end, but he has *always* been defeated.

Rise up! Rise up! Rise up! Speak to our spirit to rise. Rise up in our spirit. Announce the defeat of the enemy. No matter what our physical eye sees our spirit eyes see with much more truth. Announce truth from our spirit.

———·———

Chapter 23

The Angel of Inventory

We had just moved into a new home and the following morning after the move, I heard these instructions in my journaling time:

> *Remember to call upon the Angel of Inventory. He knows where everything was placed—EVERYTHING. Acquaint yourself with him and his function. Just like other things in Heaven, Heaven has lists of everything that you packed and where it was placed. Heaven does this for every believer as well.*
>
> *To know where things disappeared to is helpful and helps to alleviate stress that can occur when you cannot recall where something was packed. He can highlight the box, give an image of the item being placed in a box or other container, and even provide you with an inventory list of each container. It is not hard for Heaven to provide these things to the sons and daughters as the*

Father wants His sons and daughters to be able to rest in their journey. Remember, in John 14:2, 'In my Father's house are many roadside stations,' (ARTB). These are resting places on a journey just as you used to see on the roadways of your nation where picnic tables were provided for enjoyment and to provide a resting place. Then you had the small motels and cabins that provided a place for overnight lodging.

The Father is all about rest
and not about stress or striving.

He does not want that for His sons and daughters as it damages their bodies and emotional state. He wants them to live in health and wholeness. Fullness of joy is their portion.

Ask the Angel of Inventory to guide you to where the things you have need of were placed. Pay attention to the nudges you will experience for they will often be quite gentle. It is a co-laboring with the angels that Father is building with His sons and daughters, and you get to participate in it. The final part of that is if you are having trouble receiving the information, access a seer and the seer gift. They can help.

——— · ———

Chapter 24
Our Living Calendar

The instruction from Heaven was "Speak faith to your calendar." We had been working on scheduling for an upcoming meeting and had been introduced to our calendar. Our calendar is a living being—not static as we might suppose. The tips we learned from Heaven will help all of you as well.

> *When accessing the Business Complex to view our business or ministry calendar, we need to understand that it is not a static, dead thing, but it is a living being.*

I describe it as the characters in the animated Disney movie *Beauty and the Beast*, where the teapot and the candlestick were alive and moving. It appears like that, only not necessarily in an animated fashion.

Because it is living, we can interact with it. When we discuss our calendar, we release faith-filled words over it. We 'word-seed' it and some of the seeds will take off and begin to grow. Those are the ones we will cultivate. We discussed potential dates for the upcoming meeting and we word-seeded those dates and they began to grow. From the optional dates, one looked more promising. We began to see this in our calendar. We were told to ask, in this and in future situations, "What begins to grow? What begins to take root?" Wouldn't we then cultivate the seedling that looks the healthiest? We noticed that one seedling did not get to take root, or it did not get as much root as the others based on the words spoken over it. As we continued to discuss this with those involved in the process, we saw the word related to the "when" for the meeting begin to grow. It took on more vigor. Because of that enlargement, it would be the one to go. It was done by bathing a word-seed. Also, the impression of Holy Spirit will bring our mind to a conclusion as well, like we knew to wait and not make any plans until we heard something.

———·———

Chapter 25
New Angelic Tools

We engaged with Ezekiel and he showed how he had been roping storms. He showed a light gray thing that looked like a whirlwind or tornado. He was holding a lariat that he had been using to rope the whirlwinds and collapse them. He reminded us to commission angels to collapse storms.[20] He implored us, "Do not forget, you can do this more. Do not forget it. Do not forget it. Do not forget it."

In response we immediately paused and said,

We freshly commission you Ezekiel to do as you have been doing to collapse storms around LifeSpring International Ministries, its staff, its clients, its equipment, those we trade with, its outlets, and its times.

---

[20] See the chapter on Collapsing Storms.

We commission you to collapse all storms that have been raised up by demons or those operating with demons.

We commission you to collapse the storms, to bring them to zero, to flatten them, to remove their frequencies. We ask you to do this in every element and spiritual dimension and physical dimension of those associated with LifeSpring International Ministries, all people on staff, all clients, all students, all our equipment, all our possessions, all our spiritual portals, all our sensing, all our travel, and our finances. We commission you and ask you to collapse these storms. Collapse the storms around our bodies, and the health of our bodies. Collapse the storms, remove the frequencies, and defeat darkness.

We commission you, your commanders, and your ranks to this in the name of Jesus Christ.

Ezekiel reminded us to not disrobe from our garments of righteousness but wear the breastplate of righteousness. We are to wear His garment of righteousness. We **are** the righteousness of God in Christ Jesus. Wear it. Put it on. Take it up. Do not leave it in the closet. Think from the mentality of the righteousness of God who lives in us. We are righteous. All of Heaven sees our righteousness in Jesus.

His righteousness is worn by His sons and daughters.

The family of God wearing the righteousness of God is the remnant of God, having been fully redeemed to the true knowledge of their righteousness as sons and daughters. Remember, righteousness trumps and rules over darkness. It emanates a stronger, fuller velocity of power than darkness. Do not be deceived. Light rules over dark. Righteousness rules over evil. Wear righteousness.

Watch our mouth in this. We must exceedingly guard our lips that we speak the righteousness of God into situations, into circumstances, into developments, into the crashing waves of what God is bringing. Speak the righteousness of God into circumstances. Let us loose the word "righteousness" into our circumstances.

It's like this: we see a circumstance and we simply stand our ground and from the spirit and from Heaven down we speak, "I release righteousness to this situation. I release the righteousness of God to this circumstance. I release the righteous wrath of God to this situation, and I call alongside the righteous armies of God to insert righteousness into this timeline in Jesus' name."

Lightning Bolts

When we release righteousness into a circumstance, an angel takes what looks like a piece of white lightning with the zigzag we typically see in drawings of lightning bolts and they throw the lightning bolts like a javelin. Sense the power of that.

> *When the lightning bolt is released,*
> *it causes people to vibrate differently.*

When released, it is a light power that is inserted into a situation, and it changes the frequency that has boiled up. We are not loosing it to a person, we are *loosing it to a circumstance* because the enemy is manipulating from the second heaven realms a deception, a veil, or a blanket. These are ways we say an enemy plan is afoot, so the righteous can then release the righteousness of God into a circumstance. The spirit realm wars with spirit tools, with spiritual tools, and the lightnings of God is a spiritual tool.

> *He fills his hands with lightning bolts*
> *and hurls each at its target.*[21]

Do not forget, we must release with faith. We *must* release it with faith. If we are just loosing it with our language, our verbiage, we are not engaged rightly. Raise our spirit higher to the third Heaven realm and release from there. Release when our spirit is forward because our spirit is engaged *with* faith.

---

[21] Job 36:32

Fog Dispeller

Further into our engagement with Ezekiel, we requested of him what he might need. He mentioned more rope, elixir, and practice targets. Ezekiel had been working with some of the ranks with practice targets. Then he showed us what looked like a tear gas cannister. We asked what it was, and he called it a "Fog Dispeller," whose purpose was to dispel fog from the enemy that has cloaked things and made them hard to see.

Fog Dispeller helps the people of God see what the enemy does not want them to see.

If people would arm their angels with fog dispeller, they must be prepared not to agree with fear or hatred when the fog is removed because something will be exposed. We must remember that our battle is not with humanity. It is with darkness. It is with Satan's forces. We will see the exposé of something for the purpose of prayer and bringing it into righteousness and bringing it into alignment, but fog dispeller is needed by God's people because they need to see what Satan does not want them to see. We are in a season in which we need things to be exposed.

The purpose of exposure is to bring light to something.

We then requested the rope and elixir for Ezekiel, his commanders, and ranks, and we also requested Fog Dispeller for them and practice targets. We instructed,

We commission you to freely use the fog dispeller so that we might see what the enemy does not want us to see.

Ezekiel suggested that we tell this to the Senior Advocates so that they could arm the angels of his ranks with Fog Dispeller during a session if they suddenly feel like they need more sight or need to see with more clarity.

Chapter 26

The Eye Salve

As we engaged Heaven one day, we were shown by Lydia what looked like a round jar of ointment. It was eye salve which we had been gifted from the Father. A new eye salve was being released from Heaven for those who operate in our ministry. It was for both seeing and renewing seeing. It works to help one see more broadly.

I began to envision the various lenses used in professional photography. To see more broadly, one would use a wide-angle lens, for example. This eye salve also helps one focus, more narrowly when focus is needed to see a fine detail. This is much like a macro lens which we use on a camera when we want to look at the details of a flower; we use the macro lens and it brings the image up close. Again, to see more broadly, to see what is at the periphery, we would use a wide-angle lens like when we want to see a whole stadium full of people and we are standing at the 50-yard line. For the ability to focus down to the one who is selling popcorn in the stands, we would use a zoom lens.

This eye salve also contains a discernment—the discerning knowledge of the will of the Father. To discern the will of the Father in conjunction with what one is seeing is a high-level operation of seeing in the spirit and ministering from that perspective. Jesus ministered from this perspective in His ministry.

The eye salve looked like crushed diamonds in a fine powdery-pasty form mixed with oil. It was an ointment and was spreadable, but it looked like crushed diamonds and a mixture of some sort of an opalescence oil. We can apply it to our eyes. It works at night when we are asleep, when our conscience is asleep, when our soul is resting and asleep, our spiritual sight is still active—it is still seeing with discernment of knowledge.

How did the first church in the upper room discern the flaming tongues of fire? By their spirit sight—it was a gift at Pentecost. Our angel(s) will help us know how to distribute it to others that we minister to. They will be present for the administration of it.

There is an unlimited quantity. Many have not known to ask, but more importantly, many have not been aligned with a visionary ministry who is talking about the invitation to the sons of God to open their eyes and see. "OPEN YOUR EYES AND SEE" is the name of the ointment. This is ointment needed for the sons and daughters—OPEN YOUR EYES AND SEE. The Father desires all his children to see. Go read the stories in scripture of those born blind and see Jesus' ministry to them. The Father desires none of his children to be born blind (as in born again blind). That would be so wrong.

The Father desires all His children to see. He desires that they not be born again blind but born again seeing and experiencing the activation of seeing.

The activation of seeing is for when one sees one can speak what one sees.

This is the activity of the sons of God. Look at Jesus—He saw what the Father was doing, and He announced, spoke, released, directed, and/or instructed from His knowledge of what He saw the Father doing. Another way to say this is that He saw what was coming out of Heaven's realm that was available to the earth realm for the moment. He could see this as what His Father's Kingdom was about. Then He voiced it, spoke it into being, and released it into the earth realm by His agreement.

First one sees, then one voices what is seen it to give release.

We often do this as we see the will of the Father in a court scenario, and work to gain our petition before the judge, knowing the outcome of freedom that we are in the court to achieve. Ministering in this way is a sure gratification of hope.

With a puzzled look, we noticed two names on the label of the eye salve. "OPEN YOUR EYES AND SEE" was one name and as Lydia turned the jar around, we could see another label with the title, "Look! Look! Look!"

---

*The ointment had two names because one is the name of the **ability** while the other is the name of the **activity**.*

We could also say it this way: one is *the name of the purpose*, and the other is *the name of the activation*. The 'Look! Look! Look!' *is the activation* and this is for ministry. We were instructed that it is for *this* ministry to continue to minister to those who come near first. Their need in this hour is to open their eyes and see. The next need is to be activated. That would be the purpose. Then the activation is the 'Look! Look! Look!'"

The ointment helps ease the way of the activation when shared with others.

Remember the story of Naaman where he was told how to cleanse the leprosy? He was told how to do it; he was told to go to the Jordan River and dip in the water seven times—it is like that. There is the gift of it called "Open Your Eyes and See," but it is linked to an activation, and both are required to receive it and operate in it. The "Look! Look! Look!" is the activity of the son or daughter of God once they have received the eye salve.

When we administer this, people are going to see. Be prepared to write, write, write. Be prepared to record, record, record. Be prepared to learn, learn, learn. We must get activated in it with the look, look, look, but then we must learn to steward it. We must learn to discipline the gift we have to learn when to use it, when to do it, who to do it with, how to do it, why we are doing it.

---
*Our motivation must be pure
and from righteousness.*

The five W's and the how, the when, the where, the why, the what and the who is the stewardship of it.

---
*This cannot be done outside
of connection with God.*

It must be done IN connection and IN relationship with Him. It is for looking into Kingdom realms, looking into God's heavenly realms—third heaven realms.

This is like dreams in that we had to learn the type, the flavor, and the expression of the dream and whether the dream was for a now interpretation, a later interpretation, or an unknown interpretation. We learn to trust God that He is the director of that part of it, and if it is a now interpretation, we work to get it and we *will* get it. If it is for later or a hidden one, we wait on it and when its time comes, we will have it. This is similar.

It is like learning to be the steward of the gift. Isn't that what God gave the sons of God to do, to steward from the earth all that was before them as His sons and daughters? We must have Jesus as an example, we must follow our big brother in this, because Satan wants this ability, and he is mad that we have it.

———·———

Chapter 27

Working with Our Assignments

As we stepped into Heaven to find out what we were to talk about one evening on the LifeSpring Mentoring group, we could hear all kinds of musical sounds. These were happy sounds—they just made our spirit happy.

Heaven wanted us to experience the joy sounds of heaven—the joy of celebration, the joy of Jesus's beauty, the joy of His success, the celebration of His courts. We need to know that we can come to Heaven to receive this sound of Heaven. We suffer because we lack seeking after the Kingdom of God. This is seeking after the Kingdom of God, when our soul is stepped back, our body is relaxed, and our spirit man is forward, ascending through Heaven to hear the heavenly sounds.

The sounds of Heaven may be felt before they are heard. We could also hear people laughing and talking and learn that it was the sound of Heaven's fellowship; enjoy enjoying the presence of the Son. His presence is everywhere in Heaven. We easily enjoy His presence. *We can come and easily enjoy His presence*. We lose out because we do not step into Heaven and hear those heavenly sounds.

The atmosphere then shifted to a more quiet, sober, and serene atmosphere within a different area of the heavenly realm. It was explained that this was the sereneness of purpose. What we sensed was the subtraction of busy-ness. It was the flow of purpose. It had things to do, things to accomplish, and places to be, but it did not hold distraction and it did not hold busy-ness. It did not hold anxiety. It did not hold anxiety about the outcome. It held faith and belief in a good outcome. This was His presence as well for the increase of His Glory on the earth to be at peace and operate from peace. Peace is a strength of Heaven, and we can engage this peace from our spirit—from our spirit man.

Sometimes, humanity in the Body of Christ is trying to do the work that angels are supposed to do, and we get in a state of anxiety. The angels are supposed to war on our behalf, and we are supposed to direct them and co-labor and work with them. We simply must believe that they are capable and do not need our help to conduct warfare except to do what we are appointed to do.

When people find out about demonic entities, such as Leviathan, they begin to wonder and have some curiosity about it, and they step over into alignment with Leviathan and that is not good. We can know about it, but we need not know *everything* about it or worry about it. We simply need to just put angels to work about it. Call our angels near and let our angels step in. We are not meant to fight against Leviathan so let the angels of the Host fight through the angelic network.

When Ezekiel tells us that he has been working against Leviathan in victory, any anxiety we feel is because we have overstepped into thinking we need to do something about that when it is Ezekiel that does something about that. We just direct him and see what he needs—see what the victory is and continue to encourage him in his activity against Leviathan. Remember, Leviathan is a defeated spirit. It is an absolutely defeated spirit. What humans do is they think about that spirit and forget that it is defeated, and it grows. The deception is that it will grow in their mind as an undefeated spirit when it is *totally* defeated. It knows it is defeated, but it is counting on the fact that we forget that and that we do not know it is defeated and then it can work against us. It works through deception, so we must be very discerning about it.

We must think of these spiritual entities that have been defeated as very small, because they are all small.

What they do is they project themselves as large, as impenetrable, as impossible. They are lying. They are deceiving us. We are greater than they are. We are more powerful than they are in Jesus. We have a bigger projection than they do because we project from the realm of the Kingdom of God. However, when we forget that and just do it from our humanity, from the physical plane, then we are unequally matched, but angels are NOT unequally matched. Do not let the enemy project his largeness to us when he is little and under our feet.

Receiving Assignments

Now let's talk about assignments. The people of God who are seeking the Kingdom are the ones who receive assignments. The people of God who have not yet learned to seek for the Kingdom of God are not receiving assignments from Heaven, instead they are making them up and assuming that there is an assignment when there is not. This causes the Body of Christ to suffer needlessly. An assignment from Heaven can be known when we seek the Kingdom. We can step into the realms of heaven and ask if there is an assignment for us, or Holy Spirit can give us the unction that we have an assignment.

Assignments are activities—sometimes of words, and sometimes a deed. They work to bring the peace of God to the earth. They work to bring the manifestation of the principles of the Father to earth. They often have signs that follow them.

When one completes an assignment or is working through an assignment in faith, there are many signs along the way to confirm, but assignments are spiritual things. They come from Heaven. They do not come from the earth realm. They do not come from the intellect. They do not come from thinking it up.

Assignments can be found in the Court of Records. Saints can enter the Court of Records and find out if there is an assignment list and what is at the top. Some saints may be surprised by what is at the top of their assignment list.

Assignments from Heaven come with timing, so if we have missed an assignment, it may no longer be on our assignment list because the timing for that in our lives has passed. Heaven knows that we are in time. Heaven knows that we are in geographical space. Being led by the assignments of Heaven make for a richness in one's life, because it is a spiritual assignment that the spirit receives.

> *The spirit gets the agreement of the soul and the body to carry the assignment out.*

The spirit must be forward and receiving the flow of Heaven to continue.

Assignments come and go. They are not static. They have a flow to them in time and space and we can miss an assignment if we are not in the right timing. These assignments can be with others, they can be with teams, or they can be solo assignments.

With the assignments of Heaven, we can get an assignment or an inclination of an assignment in a dream. We can get an inclination of an assignment by listening to Holy Spirit in our quiet time, or in our journaling time, or by praying in tongues. If our spirit is focused on what Heaven is doing, even if our soul is in front, our spirit knows that our soul is in front, doing something very necessary like caring for a child or caring for an elderly parent. If our spirit is also focused on Heaven because we have had quiet time to get that assignment, then during our day our spirit relates to the Spirit of God. Even when our soul is doing things, our spirit man is going to know when to break in to do an assignment.

Some of these things are prayer, or kindness, or the release of language to another human. Living by the function of the spirit is another way to say this. This gets settled in our day when we open our day in some manner of seeking after God and giving ourselves permission that our spirit is going to abide with the Spirit of God all day, and our soul is giving permission to our spirit to come forward and break through at any time. Our soul and our spirit are divinely matched. They should work beautifully together in a flow in which one of them needs to be in operation in the moment.

The trouble for many humans is the distraction of the physical plane, the intentional distractions within the world systems, and the capturing of our attention through witchcraft, pharmakeia, wounding, and the activity of demons—all these things distract.

Let me explain what I mean by "capture our spirit." Our spirit itself is not captured, but its *attention* is captured—its ability to flow with God, to thrive in the presence. It is never away from us so much as it is just turned to look at these other powerful things that are gaining its attention. What happens is the soul then compensates and takes on a double-duty and tries to be both the spirit *and* the soul. The spirit of a man is refreshed in heavenly places, by the Spirit of God and by ministering angels, but it also can be disciplined to direct that person's life. It is a spiritual discipline. It is a work of pausing to determine what part of me should be working right now. What part of me should be presenting up front right now? There are times of the day, where it is really primed for our spirit to be receiving from Holy Spirit and many do not do that. Therefore, many are sad, they are sick, they are hopeless, and they are purposeless, because *our assignment* and *our purpose* come from Heaven.

Little pieces of assignment make up the whole of one's purpose.

It flows in throughout one's lifetime. There are times when it is seasons, it is cycles, it is times of the day, times of the week, times of the month, and times of the year. It is where our blessing from Heaven is so available if we will merely tune our spirit and receive.

These are also the times where the enemy is at work to deflect, divert, and disengage us from our primary lifegiving moments of spirit to Spirit and operating and working from heavenly realms. The continuation of learning to live spirit-forward continues and must be practiced and advanced. When we feel stuck, we must learn to ask our angels to come near to help us and they will.

Assignments can also come from messenger angels. These are for the mature saints, and by mature, I mean those who are several years on the planet, as well as the number of times spent in the presence and seeking heavenly realms.

Wider portals are opening for this even now in the earth—wider portals and more saints operating from their spirit. All of this is going to bring Heaven closer to earth.

About Resistance

I want to talk about resistance for a moment. Satan and his demons will work to resist us from operating in our spirit. If we do not know that, then we are going to let his lazy efforts keep us from being spirit forward—and he is very lazy.

The primary thing he will project to us is that *this is too hard*. The second thing he will use is *others are better than me at this. I will just leave it to them*. When we fall for these things, the kingdom of darkness wins in that moment, so do not be like that. Be assured and confident that we are competent, that we are a spirit being, that we have spiritual access to the Father, the Son, the Holy Spirit, angels, the cloud of witnesses, heavenly realms, and that this is meant for us. Then practice, practice, practice. Make time to pause. It will be surprising even if we pause for just 10 minutes and seek the Kingdom for 10 minutes, how it will change our morning or our afternoon, even amid clamoring distractions and natural things that must be taken care of.

Here are some of the lies:

- I cannot do that.
- There is too much going on.
- I cannot do this now because I am no good at it.
- I cannot pause and get into the presence and be in spiritual realms even for 10 minutes, because there is no time.

These are some of the lies of the enemy and we must surmount them. We must overcome them. We must leap over them. Stand on top of them, rise over them, conquer them, put them under our feet, and see how small and inadequate and piddly they are. Our practice at doing that a couple of times in a row in a season is going to really help our soul to step back, sit down, and rest, and our spirit and our lives will be enriched.

Quite honestly, we need to encourage each other in this. We need to encourage one another to be spirit forward. We need to talk about the enemy's lies and his distractions. We need to help each other understand when they have fallen into a pattern of being diverted, discouraged, and distracted, so we can encourage one another to break out by getting in the presence, getting into our secret place, and getting there in a consistent manner. Recognize that Heaven knows when we are attempting to do this, and Heaven is trying to help us. If we have time for 10 minutes or 15 minutes, that is much better than *no* minutes.

Let this be the biggest encouragement we give the Body of Christ. Two minutes, five minutes, 10 minutes, 18 minutes of being in heavenly places, seeking the Kingdom of God, and stepping into the realms of Heaven is so much better than *NO* minutes.

Let me give this word: "Surmount." Say, "I will surmount the distractions. I will surmount the diversions. I will surmount and seek the Kingdom of God. Surmount and seek the Kingdom of God!"

Chapter 28

Epilogue

In May of 2021, my wife and I moved to Pinehurst, North Carolina, a few miles from where I grew up. During the time of preparation for the move, I had been given a brief respite from writing. However, one morning shortly after returning from a ministry engagement out of state, I was impressed that it was time to put together the content for the next book, *Engaging Heaven for Revelation – Volume 2*.

The first volume had been published at the beginning of 2021, so it did not take long before we had received enough content through our regular engagements with Heaven to support a second volume of revelations we received while engaging with Heaven. The subject matter of this book is as varied as it was in the first volume. We had engaged with Lydia, Ezekiel, Mitchell, Garzan, Malcolm and many others. We also had a special visit from Abraham who spoke to us on the subject of surrender.

In the convening months since the first volume, we have heard and read many testimonies of the benefits received from these revelations. We trust that you have benefited from the revelations unveiled in this volume. May your time with Heaven be richer and your life as a son or daughter of God be fuller, sweeter, and more impactful than ever before. We bless you in that regard, in Jesus' name.

———·———

Appendix

Learning to Live Spirit First

A challenge with how we were taught about the Christian life is that everything was put off until sometime in the future. Then, we read the letters of Paul and we experienced a disconnect. Heaven, to us, was a destination, not a resource. We knew nothing about learning to live from our spirits. We only knew what we had been doing all our lives, since birth, and that is to live to satisfy our soul or our flesh. We sorely need to learn an alternative way of living.

Exchanging Our Way of Living

Paul recorded these words in his letter to the Romans:

Those who are motivated by the flesh only pursue what benefits themselves. But those who live by the impulses of the Holy Spirit are motivated to pursue spiritual realities. (Romans 8:5)

We must learn to live spirit first! We must exchange our way of living. We must learn to live from our spirit. We need to understand the hierarchy within us:

- We are a spirit.
- We possess a soul.
- We live in body.

Each component has a specific purpose in our lives. Our spirit is the interface with the supernatural realm. It is designed for interfacing with Heaven & the Kingdom realm. Our spirit has been in existence in our body since our conception. Our soul has a different purpose. It communicates to our intellect and our physical body what our spirit has obtained from Heaven. It is the interface with our body. Our body houses the two components and will follow the dictates of whichever component is dominating,

Most of us have never been taught about having our spirit dominate. Rather, we have merely assumed that our soul being dominant was the required mode of operation.

Our soul always wants to be in charge. Our soul is susceptible to carnal or fleshly desires, lusts, and behaviors. It will, at times, resist our spirit and body. It must be made to submit to our spirit by an act of our will.

Our will is a means of instructing either component (spirit, soul, or body) what to do. Our soul has a will and so does our spirit. We *choose* which part dominates!

Our body, on the other hand, has appetites that will control us in subjection to our soul. They become partners in crime—remember that second piece of chocolate cake it wanted? Our body will try, along with our soul, to dictate our behavior. It will resist the spirit's domination of our lives. However, it will obey our spirit's domination if instructed, and our body can aid our spirit if trained to do so.

The typical expression that operates in most people's lives is that their soul is first, body second, and their spirit is somewhere in the distance in last place.

In some people, especially those very conscious of their physical fitness or physical appearance, there is a different lineup. Their body is their priority, the soul second, and again their spirit is the lowest priority.

Heaven's desire for us is vastly different. Heaven desires that we live spirit first, soul second, and body third. Since we are spiritual beings, this is the optimal arrangement. For most of us, our spirit was not activated in our lives in any measure until we became born again.

If, after our salvation experience, we began to pursue our relationship with the Father, then we became much more aware of our spirit and learning to live more spirit conscious. The apostle Paul wrote in his various epistles about living in the spirit or walking in the spirit.

> *Because we are spiritual beings,*
> *our spirits cry out for a deepening*
> *of relationship with the Father.*

Our spirit longs for it and will try to steer us in that direction.

Our soul has certain characteristics that explain its behavior in our lives. This is the briefest of lists, but I think we will get the idea. Our soul is selfish. It wants what it wants when it wants it. It can be very pouty. It can act like a small child. It is offendable and often even looks for opportunities to be offended. Our soul is also rude.

Our body has a distinct set of characteristics. It is inconsiderate, demanding, lazy, and self-serving. It does not want to get out of bed in the morning, for many people. In others, it wants to be fed things that are not beneficial.

However, characteristics of our spirit are hugely different. If we live out of our spirit, we will find that we are loving and prone to be gentle. We desire peace. We are considerate. We are far more contented when living out of our spirit. Also, joy will often have great expression in our lives.

Sometimes we have experienced traumas that create a situation of our soul not trusting our spirit. The soul blames the spirit for not protecting it. The irony is that typically, our soul never gave place to the spirit so that it could protect us. The soul places false blame on the spirit and it must be coerced to forgive the spirit. Then the soul must relinquish control to the spirit. Once the soul forgives the spirit, the two components can begin to work in harmony.

If I were to flash an image of some delicious, freshly cooked donuts in front of us, what would happen? For many, our body would announce a craving for one. What if, instead, I showed an image of a bowl of broccoli? How many people would get excited about that? Not as much excitement would be experienced over a bowl of broccoli. Which does our body prefer—the donuts or the broccoli? For the untamed soul, the donuts are likely to win out every time. Which do most kids prefer?

In any case, we can train ourselves to go for the healthier option. A principle regarding this that I heard years ago is summed up like this:

What we feed will live—
what we starve will die

What do we want to be dominant—our spirit, our soul, or our body? The part we feed is the part that will dominate.

For some, they feed their soul and live by the logic of their mind. Everything must be reasoned out in their mind before they will accept it. However, because our soul gains its insight from the Tree of the Knowledge of

Good and Evil, it will always have faulty and limited understandings.

How do we change this soul-dominant or body-dominant pattern? We instruct our soul to back up and we call our spirit to come forward. Some people may need to physically stand up and speak to our soul and say, "Soul, back up," and as they say those words, take a physical step backward. Then, speak to their spirit aloud and say, "Spirit, come forward." As we speak those words, take a physical step forward. This prophetic act helps trigger a shift within them.

Live spirit first!

Benefits of Living Spirit First

Why would we want to live spirit first? Let me present several reasons to us. Living spirit first will create in us an increased awareness of Heaven and the realms of Heaven. It will create a deeper comprehension of the presence of Holy Spirit, and of angels and men and women in white linen. We will be able to better hear the voice of Heaven. We will experience greater creativity, productivity, hope, and peace. We will become more aware of the needs of people that we can meet.

As we live spirit first, we will be able to access the riches of Heaven in our lives. Petty things that formerly bothered us will dissipate in importance or impact in our lives. We will be able to move ahead, not concerning ourselves with the petty, mundane, or unproductive things that have affected our lives before we began to live spirit first.

This way of life is more than a game changer—for the believer, it is the only way to live. We *will* face challenges as we build our business or live our lives from Heaven down, but we will more readily be able to access the solutions of Heaven as we live with an awareness of the richness of Heaven and all that is available to us as a son or daughter of the Lord Most High. Do not live dominated by the soul. *Live spirit first!*

———·———

Works Cited

Strong, J. (n.d.). *Strong's Concordance.*

Description

More Riches from Heaven

The flow of revelation from Heaven is increasing daily. As more of the sons of God awaken to who they are portals will open throughout the earth with the result being more of Heaven flooding the earth. Regardless of our church tradition, we have been taught to pray, "Your Kingdom come, Your will be done on earth as it is in Heaven." The bowls of intercession are now overflowing, and the result is the outpouring of revelation. More angelic activity is occurring in the earth right now than at any time previous. We can learn to engage Heaven for revelation and be forever changed. This is the second volume in this series by Dr. Ron M. Horner. May it bless your life.

———·———

About the Author

Dr. Ron Horner is an apostolic teacher specializing in the Courts of Heaven. He has written over twenty books on the Courts of Heaven, Engaging Heaven, working with angels, or living from revelation.

He currently trains people in engaging the Courts of Heaven in a weekly online teaching session. You can register to participate and discover more about the Courts of Heaven prayer paradigm through his various websites, classes, products, and services found here:

www.ronhorner.com

———·———

Other Books by Dr. Ron M. Horner

Building Your Business from Heaven Down

Building Your Business from Heaven Down 2.0

Building Your Business with the Blueprint of Heaven

Commissioning Angels – Volume 1

Cooperating with The Glory

Courts of Heaven Process Charts

Dealing with Trusts & Consequential Liens from the Courts of Heaven

Engaging Angels in the Realms of Heaven

Engaging Heaven for Revelation – Volume 1

Engaging Heaven for Revelation – Volume 2

Engaging Heaven for Trade

Engaging the Courts for Ownership & Order

Engaging the Courts for Your City (*Paperback, Leader's Guide & Workbook*)

Engaging the Courts of Healing & the Healing Garden

Engaging the Courts of Heaven

Engaging the Help Desk of the Courts of Heaven

Engaging the Mercy Court of Heaven

Four Keys to Dismantling Accusations

Freedom from Mithraism

Kingdom Dynamics – Volume 1

Kingdom Dynamics – Volume 2

Let's Get it Right!

Lingering Human Spirits

Lingering Human Spirits – Volume 2

Living Spirit Forward

Overcoming the False Verdicts of Freemasonry

Overcoming Verdicts from the Courts of Hell

Releasing Bonds from the Courts of Heaven

Unlocking Spiritual Seeing

SPANISH

Cómo Proceder en la Corte Celestial de Misericordia

Las Cuatro Llaves para Anular las Acusaciones

Liberando Bonos en las Cortes Celestiales

Liberando Su Visión Espiritual

Sea Libre del Mitraísmo

Tablas de Proceso de la Cortes del Cielo

Viviendo desde el Espíritu

www.ingramcontent.com/pod-product-compliance
Lightning Source LLC
Chambersburg PA
CBHW022005160426
43197CB00007B/287